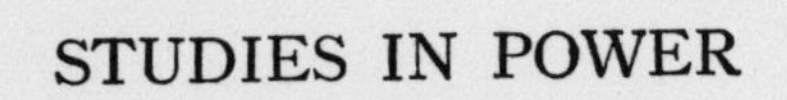

STUDIES IN POWER

STUDIES IN POWER

By
HENRY M. EDMONDS

COKESBURY PRESS
NASHVILLE, TENN.
1931

STUDIES IN POWER

C

Printed in the United States of America

DEDICATION

DEDICATED TO A RIVER, FULL OF MOODS AND CONSOLATIONS AS A WOMAN, AND SOMETIMES WEARING A VEIL OF MIST; FULL OF LIGHT AND HEALING; COOLER THAN THE DAY—OR WARMER; DEEPLY MYSTERIOUS; BABBLING SECRETS ALL DAY LONG; SINGING ALL NIGHT; GREEN AND DARKLING UNDER THE SUN, HOLDING TREES UPSIDE DOWN; AT NIGHT A WINDING LANE OF LIGHT AND, UNDER THE MOON, SILVER; IN WHOSE PRESENCE CHILDREN LAUGH AND THE OLD FIND THEIR BURDENS GONE; STRETCHES ENDING IN A BANK OF GREEN OR A WALL OF ROCK, YET ALWAYS FINDING A WAY THROUGH; A SMALL RIVER, FRIENDLY, INTIMATE, REFRESHING, RENEWING; PICTURE OF GOD'S LIFE IN THE WORLD AND OF HIS HEAVEN HEREAFTER; AND OF THE SPIRIT OF MAN, FOREVER COURSING THROUGH THE OLD, YET FOREVER SEEKING THE NEW, SIMPLE, MAJESTIC, UNSTABLE YET MIGHTY, WINDING OUT FROM GOD AND BACK AGAIN—

THE LITTLE CAHABA

CONTENTS

INTRODUCTION

THIS is a religious book. Nor is its conclusion tacked on to make it so. It would be anyway. Indeed, it is much more religious than I had thought it would be.

My original idea was simply to inquire into the secrets of the power by which certain men and women had influenced the thoughts and acts of others. Only indirectly would that be religious, I imagined, since it could do no more than furnish suggestions by which life in all its phases might be made more effective. I found immediately, however, that in each case I was inevitably judging men by the standards established in the life and character of Jesus. I found, in the second place, that each subject was an exhibit in the study of the progress of religious ideas—in other words, that Church History and Theology are after all biographical, that only people count; and not special people, like religious leaders, but the ordinary run of people—just people. Next, I found that those individuals—prominent in world affairs but just people in matters of religion—were in most cases intensely, and often beautifully, religious. Lastly, I found myself compelled to say that the crowning secret in more than one instance was a man's faith in God.

The original selections began with Alexander the Great and sought to touch the representative races and eras since. The publishers, however, under the necessity of choice among so many, thought that a few examples in the middle period of Europe and Asia, with a larger number, comparatively, covering the American story, would be better. So I willingly followed their superior wisdom.

The American studies I had not reduced to writing, though I had delivered some of them, several times, from notes. The only available time I had for that writing and the additional reading I wanted to do was my summer vacation. The spot I chose was a one-room cabin with a screened porch, which I built four years ago on the Little Cahaba River, eight miles from Birmingham. Whether my summer there—or here, for here I am yet—has produced anything of value to others I cannot say, but to me it has been almost a pure idyl. And I hereby make acknowledgment to Mr. Horner, President of the Birmingham Waterworks Company, who gave me the privilege of building my shack on his company's property. My cooking I have done on a rough stone arrangement out in the open—and eating, too, until the yellow jackets drove me in. Early to bed and early to rise—five-fifteen about, the fire started, a dip in the rock-bound pool, my fruit, eggs, bacon, toast, George Washington coffee, then my housekeeping chores—and work. Usually by eleven-thirty I was ready for woodcutting, road building, stone hauling, repairs of one sort and another. Then another dip and lunch. Afternoons similar, though lighter. Late came my wife and some of the children, often, for a swim and supper, leavening my day and simplifying my housekeeping, not only by what they brought but by what they left. My small boy spent the week-ends with me.

And so the six weeks—rare days and nights; under great trees; beside the loveliest stream I know—clear, cool, bold, rocky, but full of friendliness; and in the midst of long deep silences.

If it isn't a good book, I am sorry, but the place is not to blame.

SEPTEMBER 10, 1930.

CHARLEMAGNE

THE Battle of Chalons in France turned back Attila and his Huns and decided the fate of Europe as Christian rather than pagan. The Germanic strain, with its capacity for self-government and its reverence for womanhood, was saved on that Flodden field by Theodoric the Goth and Aëtius the last of the Romans.

Three hundred years later another enemy threatened, this time from the south. The Mohammedan had crossed from Africa to Spain and aimed at no less than the whole of Europe. Was Europe then to be not Christian after all, but Mohammedan? Charles Martel, Charles the Hammer, Duke of the Franks, accepted the gage of battle for a Christian Europe at Tours in 732. Again destiny had spoken.

Then came Pepin. In March, 752, he was raised on a buckler by his soldiers and proclaimed King of the Franks. An old historian writes, "Pepin was proclaimed king and Childeric, who was falsely called king, was shaved and sent into a monastery." The next year Pope Stephen III needed help against the

Lombards and appealed to Pepin. Stephen visited France and, in the monastery of St. Denis, placed with his own hands the diadem on Pepin's brow, then anointed him, his wife, and children with the holy oil. Thus came into modern life the idea of the divine right of kings. "It was easy to slip those words, 'Dei Gratia,' into the coronation service. It took almost fifteen hundred years to get them out again." Pepin conquered Lombardy and assigned a part of the territory to the pope. Thus the Bishop of Rome became a temporal sovereign. Thus began the Papal State. Important things were happening in those years of the 750's.

Draper writes: "To the hilt of the sword of France the keys of St. Peter were henceforth so firmly bound that, though there have been great kings, and conquerors, and statesmen who have wielded the sword, not one to this day has been able, though many have desired, to wrench the encumbrance away." It was only in 1905 that that sword hilt and those keys were finally torn apart, after Draper's pen was still.

Pepin made the same mistake his father had made in dividing his kingdom. At his death, Charles and Carloman inherited alike. Almost immediately insurrection broke out in Aquitaine. The old duke,

Hunald, issued from his monastery in the island of Rhé to make a bid for power and independence. Charles and Carloman marched against him; but Carloman, who was hot-headed and jealous, took offense over some trifling matter and quitted the expedition with his troops. Charles continued alone with complete success. Bertha the queen-mother reconciled her two sons, but Carloman's death in two years "reëstablished unity more surely than the reconciliation had reëstablished harmony."

Charles was now in the saddle. He ought rather to be called Karl, for his blood was Germanic. Carolus Magnus was his designation in his day, for he came finally to the headship of the Roman Empire, and his culture and religion were Latin in their expression. Charlemagne he came to be and is for all time by reason of the legends that grew up about him in France. Charles the Great, as Gibbon remarks, stands alone in having his title welded to his name.

He was Charles the Great, Charlemagne, for his wars, for his government, for his patronage of learning, for the peculiar position which he came to occupy in the centuries, and for his character.

From 769 to 813, in Germany and Western and

Northern Europe, Charlemagne conducted thirty-one campaigns against the Saxons, Frisians, Bavarians, Avars, Slavs, and Danes; in Italy, five against the Lombards; in Spain, Corsica, and Sardinia, twelve against the Arabs; two against the Greeks; and three in Gaul itself, against the Aquitanians and the Bretons—in all, fifty-three expeditions.

The most difficult task Charlemagne ever set himself was the subjugation of Saxony, or what is now Germany.

"In 1772, at the general assembly of the Franks, Charlemagne 'took the resolution of going and carrying war into Saxony.' He invaded it without delay, laid it waste with fire and sword, made himself master of the fort of Ehresburg, and threw down the idol that the Saxons called Irminsul.

"The following year the Saxons entered the land of the Franks, laid them waste in their turn, and, paying back outrage for outrage, set fire to the church not long since built at Fritzlar by Boniface. The Christianity of the Franks stood thus arrayed against the national paganism of the Saxons. Whithersoever Charlemagne penetrated he built strong castles and churches; and at his departure left garrisons and missionaries. When he was gone the Saxons returned, attacked the forts, and massacred the garrisons and the missionaries."

Backward and forward, year after year, the tide of battle ebbed and flowed.

Wittikind came to the fore. He was the most formidable foe that Charlemagne ever met. As often as he was pressed he would take refuge among the Northmen to issue presently for further and more vengeful hostilities. "In 778 the Saxons advanced as far as the Rhine; but 'not having been able to cross the river,' says Einhard, 'they set themselves to lay waste with fire and sword all the towns and all the villages from the city of Duitz (opposite Cologne) as far as the confluence of the Moselle. The churches as well as the houses were laid in ruins from top to bottom. The enemy, in his frenzy, spared neither age nor sex, wishing to show thereby that he had invaded the territory of the Franks, not for plunder but for revenge!' "

Again in 782 Charlemagne's lieutenants were beaten on the banks of the Weser and the Franks almost exterminated. Swift as the news of this disaster was in reaching Charlemagne, so swift was his retribution. The Saxon chieftains agreed in denouncing Wittikind as the author of this treason; but as they could not produce him, his accomplices to the number of four thousand five hundred were placed in the hands of the king, and by his order all had their heads cut off the same day, at a place called Werden on the river Aller.

Finally Charlemagne had to take up his residence in Saxony and give all his energy to the work of conquest and conversion. "Saxony must be Christianized or wiped out," he used to say. And finally he won. Wittikind came before the king in his palace at Attigny and there received baptism.

After Saxony, Lombardy. Indeed, Lombardy meanwhile. Didier, the Lombard king, and Pope Adrian I had entered into war, and Adrian appealed to Charlemagne for help. As usual, Charlemagne sought to obtain his desires by peaceful means, but, upon Didier's refusal, he convoked the assembly of the Franks at Geneva and poured two armies into Lombardy. "One was to cross the Valais and descend upon Lombardy by Mount St. Bernard; Charlemagne in person led the other by Mount Cenis. The Lombards, at the outlet of the passes of the Alps, offered a vigorous resistance; but when the second army had penetrated into Italy by Mount St. Bernard, Didier, threatened in his rear, retired precipitately, and, driven from position to position, was obliged to go and shut himself up in Pavia, the strongest place in his kingdom, whither Charlemagne, having received on the march the submission of the principal courts and nearly all the towns of Lombardy, came promptly to besiege him."

At the close of the ninth century a monk of the Abbey of St. Gall in Switzerland had collected from the mouth of one of Charlemagne's warriors, Adalbert, numerous stories of his campaigns and his life. One of them is about his approach to Pavia and will show the impression of admiration and fear produced upon his contemporaries by Charlemagne. "Didier had with him at that time one of Charlemagne's most famous comrades, Ogier the Dane, who fills a prominent place in the romances . . . of that age. Ogier had quarreled with his great chief and taken refuge with the King of the Lombards. 'When Didier and Ogger [for so the monk calls him] heard that the dread monarch was coming, they ascended a tower of vast height whence they could watch his arrival from afar off and from every quarter. They saw, first of all, engines of war such as must have been necessary for the armies of Darius or Julius Cæsar.' 'Is not Charles,' asked Didier of Ogger, 'with this great army?' But the other answered, 'No.' The Lombard, seeing afterwards an immense body of soldiery gathered from all quarters of the vast empire, said to Ogger, 'Certes, Charles advanceth in triumph in the midst of this throng.' 'No, not yet; he will not appear so soon,' was the answer. 'What should we do then,' rejoined Didier, who began to be perturbed, 'should he come accompanied by a larger band of warriors?' 'You will see what he is when he comes,' replied Ogger, 'but as to what will become of us I know nothing.' As they were thus parleying there appeared the body of guards that knew no repose; and at this sight the Lombard, overcome with dread, cried, 'This time 'tis surely Charles.' 'No,' answered Ogger, 'not yet.' In their wake came the bishops, the abbots, the ordinaries of the chapels royal, and the counts; and then Didier, no longer able to bear the light of day or to face death, cried out with groans, 'Let us descend and hide ourselves in the bowels of the earth, far from the face and the fury of so terrible a foe.' Trembling the while, Ogger, who knew by experience what were the power and might of Charles and who had learned the lesson by long consuetude in better days, then said, 'When ye shall behold the crops shaking for fear in the fields, and the gloomy Po and the Ticino overflowing the walls of the city with their waves blackened with steel [iron], then may ye think that Charles is coming.' He had not ended these words when there began to be seen in the west, as it were a black cloud, raised by the northwest wind or by Boreas, which turned the brightest day into awful shadows. But as the emperor drew nearer and nearer, the gleam of arms caused to shine on the people shut up within the city a day more gloomy than any kind of night. And then appeared Charles himself, that man of steel, with his head encased in a helmet of steel, his hands garnished with gauntlets of steel, his heart of steel and his shoulders of marble protected by a cuirass of steel, and his left hand armed with a lance of steel which he held aloft in the air, for as to his right hand he kept that continually on the hilt of his invincible sword. The outside of his thighs, which the rest, for their greater ease in mounting a-horseback, were wont to leave unshackled even by straps, he wore encircled by plates of steel. What shall I say concerning his boots? All the army were wont to have them invariably of steel; on his buckler there was naught to be seen but steel; his horse was of the color and the strength of steel. All those who went before the monarch, all of those who marched at his side, all of those who followed after, even the whole mass of the army had armor of the like sort, so far as the means of each permitted. The fields and the highways were covered with steel; the points of steel reflected the rays of the sun; and this steel, so hard, was borne by a people with hearts still harder. The flash spread terror through the streets of the city. 'What steel! alack, what steel!' Such were the bewildered cries the citizens raised. The firmness of manhood and of youth gave way at sight of steel; and the steel paralyzed the wisdom of graybeards. That which I, pore taleteller, mumbling and toothless, have attempted to depict in a long description, Ogger perceived at one rapid glance, and said to Didier, 'Here is what ye have so anxiously sought,' and whilst uttering these words he fell down almost lifeless."

Of course Pavia fell, and Charlemagne became king of Lombardy.

Charlemagne made some expeditions against the Huns, the Avars, and the Slavs, but was content to accept tribute from them and to hold them in their boundaries, which defined on the west about what is now Russia and Southeastern Europe.

He met the great tragedy of his career in Spain. The Arabs there had fallen out among themselves, and one group appealed to Charlemagne. He accepted the summons with alacrity and again poured two armies into the territory of the enemy. Charles himself entered Spain by the valley of Roncesvalles.

He met more opposition than was expected in Spain and was apparently glad to accept indemnity of "an immense quantity of gold," hostages, and promises of homage and fidelity. Returning through the passes of Roncesvalles, his rear guard was cut off and destroyed to a man by the Basques. Roland, nephew of the king and prefect of the marches of Brittany, fell in the engagement. Einhard, who gives us the only authentic account of the Roncesvalles disaster, has little more than the above paragraph, but poetic fancy used it as a basis for one of the world's great epics. The "Song of Roland" is a real Homeric poem in beauty, rude simplicity, and primitive appeal. Two hundred and eighty-eight years later as William the Conqueror advanced to the battle of Hastings, a *jongleur* went before the army, throwing his sword in the air and singing the "Song of Roland."

"The moral influence of Charlemagne was on a par with his material power. He had everywhere protected the missionaries of Christianity; he had twice entered Rome, also in the character of protector; and he could count on the faithful support of the pope at least as much as the pope could count on him. He had received embassies and presents from the sovereigns of the East, Christian and Mussulman, from the emperors of Constantinople, and the khalifs at Bagdad. Everywhere, in Europe, in Africa, and in Asia, he was feared and respected by kings and people. Such, at the close of the eighth century, were, so far as he was concerned, the results of his wars, of the superior capacity he had displayed, and of the successes he had won and kept."

As to his government, we must remember that the Roman Empire was to all intents and purposes dead. Its achievements in government had for the time being perished from among men. Charlemagne, without the political inheritance or the political genius of the ancient Romans, set himself, however, the enormous task of organizing and governing as best he could the wide territory and the conglomerate peoples that he had conquered. His empire "comprised nearly all Germany, Belgium, France, Switzerland, and the north of Italy and Spain, . . . still . . . scarce more than the hunting ground and the battle field of all the swarms of barbarians who tried to settle on the ruins of the Roman world they had invaded and broken to pieces."

His greatness in government consists not in his success, for the structure fell to pieces at his death, but in his brave and faithful efforts to conquer the chaos about him. Even during his life he could hardly be called successful. The task was too great. It was the temporary triumph of an absolute but beneficent monarchy.

In broad outline his government had four parts:

1. The dukes, with auxiliary officers, residing on the spot, appointed by the emperor and in his name levying troops, rendering justice, maintaining order, and receiving imposts.

2. The vassals of the emperor, who held lands as his gift and exercised a certain jurisdiction over such areas.

3. Above these agents, local and resident, Charlemagne appointed *missi dominici,* temporary commissioners, to inspect the condition of the provinces. They went from place to place, correcting abuses and rendering account to their master.

4. Finally there were the general assemblies of the people. Thirty-five of these are counted from

the years 770 to 813. At least at one time they came regularly twice a year. They were called March parades and May parades and must have been partially military in character, though mainly political. It was the people's opportunity to talk, to report trouble, to ask redress, to initiate reforms. The emperor submitted laws, and the grandees sat in council upon them. Amendments and suggestions were made, but the emperor had the final word. "With him rests will and motive, initiative and decision."

Many of the laws of Charlemagne have come down to us under the title of Capitularies (small chapters, articles). These are of the widest variety. Some of them are not laws at all, but instructions and injunctions about many matters. "Hospitality must be practiced," for example. Another is: "Let none suppose that prayer cannot be made to God save in three tongues, for God is adored in all tongues, and man is heard if he do but ask for the things that be right." Beggars who will not work are not to be helped. He regulates Church and State alike. "No bishops, abbots, priests, deacons, or other members of the clergy shall presume to have dogs for hunting, or hawks, falcons, and sparrow hawks." The laws for the conquered Saxon territory are severe in the extreme and are not based on our modern ideas of personal liberty. "If anyone, out of contempt for Christianity, shall have despised the holy Lenten feast and shall have eaten flesh, let him be punished by death." The harshness of this and similar legislation is, however, considerably diminished and the influence of the Church enhanced by the discretion left to the priests in the matter of absolution.

Charlemagne was a patron of learning. "There is a list of the names and works of twenty-three men of the eighth and ninth centuries who have escaped oblivion, and they are all found grouped about Charlemagne." He formed a "school of the palace" or "academy," which followed him to his various residences, dealt with the questions he presented, and gave lessons to himself and others about the court, children and adults, in grammar, rhetoric, logic, astronomy, geometry, and theology. Alcuin, a British monk, was the director of all Charlemagne's efforts to educate his court, his children, his priests, and the people generally. "Ah," he said one day, "if only I had about me a dozen clerics learned in all the sciences as Jerome and Augustin were!" That was beyond him, but he laid the foundation of episcopal cloistral schools for the education of priests and, going yet further, he gave command to the bishops and abbots that "they should take care to make no difference between the sons of serfs and of freemen, so that they might come and sit on the same benches to study grammar, music, and arithmetic."

Charlemagne himself learned Latin and understood Greek. He strove hard to write a good hand, keeping his tablets under his pillow. He began the first Germanic grammar. He ordered that the old barbaric poems be collected for posterity. He gave Germanic names to the twelve months of the year. He distinguished the winds by twelve special terms. He paid special attention to astronomy. Some of his observations remain for us. He reformed the music in his churches, and we owe many of the Byzantine buildings still standing in the Rhineland to his encouragement of architecture. Augustine's "The City of God" is said to have been his favorite book.

I said above that Charlemagne was great by reason of the peculiar place he came to occupy among the centuries. If he had lived earlier or later, his passion for learning would not have been distinguished, but coming, as he did, after history's darkest ages, he shines like a light.

In the year 800, on Christmas Day, "he was in Rome and came into the basilica of the blessed St. Peter, apostle, to attend the celebration of mass. At the moment, when in his place before the altar, he was bowing down to pray, Pope Leo placed on his head a crown, and all the Roman people shouted, 'Long life and victory to Charles Augustus, crowned by God, the great and pacific Emperor of the Romans!' After this proclamation the pontiff prostrated himself before him and paid him adoration, according to the custom established in the days of the old emperors." At another time such exaltation might not have come to him, for there had lived stronger men than Charlemagne, and there had been mightier enemies than he had to combat, but at that particular juncture it fell to his lot to save the ruins of the Roman Empire and hold back from Europe the hordes of invaders from the east. Guizot has written, "No sovereign, no human being, perhaps, ever rendered greater service to the civilization of the world."

As a part of his great service to civilization and, in like manner, as we should say, accidentally and without any knowledge on his part of what he was doing, he became the father of modern Germany.

France, Italy, Belgium, Greece had in a manner been fathered. But Germany (Saxony, as it was then) he wrested from barbarism.

It remains to speak briefly of Charlemagne's character.

In some respects he was no model of personal morality. His first wife he divorced and in succession married eight others. At least Gibbon counts that many. I have been unable to identify the whole tally. Hildegarde, his second wife, was his life's supreme love. She died in childbirth, and her memory remains with him. There is a deed of gift to St. Arnulf of Metz of an estate for the good of her soul. To the end of time candles were to be furnished for the sepulcher of his "most beloved wife." The date is "on the day of our Lord's ascension, on the vigil of which our sweet wife passed away." But in a few months he was comforted with another wife much the inferior of Hildegarde in beauty and in character. In addition to these many wives there were also a number of marriages of the second rank, as they are euphemistically termed by his clerical admirers.

Nor can the hardness of Charlemagne's character be glossed over. He ravaged and burned and slew.

All contemporaries bear witness to the softening influence of Hildegarde. Bertha, his mother, restrained his untamed temper, too, but both voices were soon hushed. Pope Hadrian lived until 795, but already religious and political differences had estranged Charlemagne from this early mentor. Alcuin shrank aghast from some of the things he saw, but he remonstrated in vain against the Saxon and Avar policies.

The Saxon poet, writing in the last part of the ninth century, may have known Charlemagne personally. He may generously forgive the terrible preceptor of his people, but we cannot.

> "He swept away the black, deceitful night
> And taught our race to know the only Light.
> The strife was long, the peril great and sore,
> And heavy toil and sleepless watch he bore.
> But these be things all Europe has by heart;
> All Europe in that mighty work had part;
> The hosts of all his realm did he combine
> To drag this people from the devil's shrine.
> For who can turn fierce heathen from their bent
> By soft persuasion and sage argument?"

Charlemagne's cruelty is worse, not better, by reason of its usual religious purpose. Christ and compulsion God hath put asunder; let no man join them together. But we must, nevertheless, be fair. Religious liberty is a later growth. After all, men must be judged according to the standard of their times.

We cannot, however, gainsay his power. He was tall above the common; his height was seven times the length of his foot. His voice was clear, but weaker than one would have expected. He was hawk-nosed, mustached, with high forehead and shaven chin, square shouldered, and strongly built. A short, thick neck somewhat spoiled his appearance, and in later life he grew corpulent, but there was about him an innate dignity which covered these defects. Through the ballads of a later age we catch echoes of the praises of his contemporaries. He hunted the wild bull single-handed. He was so strong that he felled a horse and rider with one blow of his fist. He could straighten four horseshoes joined together and lift with his right hand a fully equipped fighting man to the level of his head. In the legends he is always drawn with a long beard and very old. The "Song of Roland" has him two hundred years old, for example. He did live to an unusually ripe age for those troublous times and to have spent himself as he did. Great conquerors are not notable for long life. Undoubtedly his age was impressive among warriors, particularly as Einhard and the Monk of St. Gall, his contemporaries who wrote most about him, were very much younger than himself.

In the minds of those who wrote and sang about him Charlemange's physical prowess was probably in part symbolic of his tireless energy, his incredible speed of movement, his flashing courage, and his iron will.

He decided, he dared, and he did. These are elements in his power.

But the most striking thing in his character, if we can judge him rightly at this distance, was his persistence, his fidelity to his task, his undiscourageable patience. His fame does not rest upon any one great battle or campaign or achievement. It was the everlasting resolution with which he kept on at the thing which he had undertaken. His biggest task was the subjugation of Saxony. He worked at it thirty-odd years. His problems in government were of the same never-ending sort, and he worked at them with the same unflagging determination. There remain to us exceedingly interesting records of the care of his estate. Every smallest thing was inventoried annually—so much linen, wool, grease, soap, honey, everything. The steward set over each property worked under the minutest regulations. Care, care, care.

Charlemagne was an executive, a manager, a husbandman, a governor, and a lover of his realm. He was faithful rather than brilliant. He built a broad, slowly emerging foundation, and, when after a while his head was thrust above the clouds, it seemed no accident or temporary thrust of straining effort.

There is a delightful sense of fundamental rightness that on the basis of such solid qualities there should have appeared one of the most luxuriant growths of legend that ever clustered about the name of any man. The "Song of Roland" has not been eclipsed in the Western world, but it is only one of a varied cycle that went all over Europe. Charlemagne became a part even of Icelandic saga. He arose from the dead and became the pattern Crusader. Joan of Arc wielded his sword.

"The Emperor spent the last weeks of the year 813 at Aachen. He occupied his time in almsgiving, in prayer, and in correcting his manuscripts of the sacred texts. Late in the month of January he was seized by a violent fever on which a pleurisy soon supervened. He had never placed his faith in physicians and now refused their advice, preferring to try his favorite remedy of starvation. This only made him weaker; on the seventh day his condition was so plainly hopeless that the arch-chaplain was called in to give him the eucharist. Next morning, a little before sunrise, he passed quietly away. His last audible words are said to have been, 'Lord, into thy hands I commend my spirit.' That same day he was buried in the church of the Virgin; we may perhaps infer from this uncourtly haste that, like his father, he had developed dropsical symptoms. Tradition affirms that he was placed on a chair of state within a little shrine or chapel of stone and that his sword Joyeuse was laid unsheathed across his knees.

Einhard has preserved the epitaph which was inscribed on a triumphal arch above the tomb: "Beneath this covering lies the body of Charles, the Great and Orthodox Emperor, who nobly enlarged the realm of the Franks and reigned happily for 47 years. He died at the age of 70, in the year of the Incarnation 814."

The lamentations of his subjects were long and loud. The Empire which he had founded was still popular; the prospect of its dissolution filled all men with dismay.

"Woe to thee, Rome, and woe to the people of Rome. The great and glorious Charles is taken from you. Woe to thee Italy, and to all thy fair cities. Many are the afflictions that Frankland has known, but never knew she such a sorrow as when at Aachen she laid in the earth the august and eloquent Charles." Such was the threnody which an obscure monk composed for him.

VLADIMIR

("The Father of Russia")

At the sound of hounds and galloping horses, Olga ran to the door. It was always a sight to see, and sights were all too scarce in that peasant cottage. Then the hunters sometimes frightened the cow away with their savage dogs, and they sometimes asked a drink and flung down a gift in exchange. The dogs ran around the house, some of the men passed, and one came steaming up who from his dress and bearing was in authority. At the sight of the girl he reined in his horse and sat staring at her. Her returning gaze was level without either boldness or self-consciousness. "Who are you?" the huntsman asked unaware that anybody else was there except himself and her. "I am Olga. Who are you?" she replied. Her voice was low and musical, and her smile like the sun breaking through a cloud. He did not reply, but rode nearer, still devouring her with his eyes, and yet not too boldly, for something in her bearing made him hesitate as he had never done before. She stood in the door unperturbed like a child. He had never seen such unaffected grace and beauty. The other men went on, snickering to themselves. And they two talked in the sun. He aimed a shaft at her as a peasant girl, which she was, but he found her as proud as himself. He attacked with intellect, but he found the cottager not less quick than the courtier. He sought to flatter, but her modesty was invincible. He left the hunt and rode back in silence, some of his men following at a distance.

Prince Igor was not to be balked of his purpose. He saw his fate and ran after it. Contrary to all advices, he honorably sought and received in marriage the lowly born yet princely-minded and lovely Olga. She left the cottage of her Norman peasant father and went to the royal castle at Kief, in March, 903.

Olga was the grandmother of Vladimir.

I wish that the picture of the peasant girl in the royal castle might remain true to the lines already sketched in, but it probably cannot. Leo, the Deacon, a Greek annalist, tells that her husband was slain by the Drevlani. Olga sought revenge. She invaded their country, and the captives she destroyed by bending two young trees together, tying a man between, and then releasing the trees to fly back and dismember the victim. Two deputations were sent to offer peace. She buried some alive and stifled others in a bathing house. She besieged their city, Korosten, which sued for peace. She demanded three pigeons and three sparrows for each house, tied lighted tow to their tails, and let them fly back to the wooden town. These stories have been told of others and may not be true. Nevertheless, they indicate the impression she was making at that time.

She was, however, a wise and beneficent ruler and gave her country years of peace. She is one of the great women of history.

But more is to happen before she is gathered to her Viking fathers. On September 9, 955, she entered Constantinople, accompanied by the nobles of her court, many ladies of distinction and the Russian ambassadors and merchants residing there. The Emperor, Constantine Porphyrogenitus, met her similarly accompanied. They proceeded to the palace, where a more than royal feast was spread in the wide banqueting hall. Richest music was provided and oriental opulence of entertainment. There was an exchange of presents, no person in either retinue suffering neglect. Then Olga was baptized into the Christian faith under the Greek name of Helen.

Her acceptance of Christianity, however, had little effect on her realm. Her own son would have none of it. "My men would despise me," he said. "And he often grew angry with her," Nestor the chronicler says.

The son came now to the throne. He is the father of Vladimir. Have a look at him. Leo, the Deacon, was close to him once at a conference with the Greek emperor and has left us his portrait. He came up in his boat, handling a paddle with the other men. "He was of middle height, but very robust, wide chest, a thick neck, blue eyes, thick eyebrows, a flat nose, long mustache, a thin beard, a tuft of hair on his shaven head as a mark of his nobility, a gold ring in one ear ornamented with a ruby and two pearls." Such was Sviatoslaf, father of Vladimir. He was a throwback to the elder Vikings. He took to the open air, taught his men to eat horseflesh, cutting it with their swords and cooking it on the naked fire. "His pillow was his saddle, his bed the earth, his curtains the sky, his covering his saddlecloth." He roamed the world in search of conquest, captured Poland, Bulgaria and contiguous territory, and threatened Constantinople. John Zimisces shut him up in Dorostol. He led his men out in wild sallies. but ineffectually. Women fought like men as in the old Scandinavian sagas. In the moonlight on nights after action the besieged stole out of the city to burn their dead. On the ashes they sacrificed prisoners of war, and drowned cocks and little children in the Danube. They killed themselves rather than surrender. Provisions failed, and they came out to fight, nailing up the gates behind them. But they had to give back, leaving 15,500 dead on the field and 20,000 shields. They swore by their gods that they would never invade again. "If we break our vows, may we become as yellow as gold and perish by our own arms."

And so home. But the Petchenegi, ancient enemies, awaited them at the rapids of the Dnieper, killed Sviatoslaf, cut off his head, and made a drinking cup out of his skull. A gold band was put around it with the inscription, "In seeking to gain the property of others thou didst lose thine own."

And now Vladimir. The kingdom was left to the three brothers. Yaropolk reigned in Kief, Oleg in the country of the Drevlians, Vladimir in Novgorod. Oleg killed the son of Sveneld when he found him hunting on his territory. The injured father stirred up Yaropolk to do battle on his behalf, and the two brothers were at war. Oleg was whipped and, fleeing with his army, fell through a bridge and was smothered under horses and men. Vladimir in fright withdrew to the farther shore of the Baltic and took refuge with the Varangians. He was there two years, participating with his Viking kinsmen in the daring enterprises that swept all the seas of Europe. Then he returned with a force of those adventurers to take back his kingdom. The representatives of his brother at Novgorod fled at his approach, with the message that he would be in Kief soon. Yaropolk was betrothed to Ragneda, beautiful daughter of Rogvolod, who ruled in Polotsk. Vladimir decided to make a clean sweep and take his brother's throne and his intended wife as well. He made the demand on the father of the girl. He, in his embarrassment, left it for her to decide. Her answer was: "I will never unboot the son of a slave," referring to the custom of the bride taking off the boots of the groom on the wedding night, and to the fact that Vladimir was the illegitimate son of a woman in waiting about the court. Vladimir was so incensed that he marched against her father, slew him and her two brothers with his own hand, and dragged her out a prisoner.

His brother, on the way to treat with him for peace, is slain by his orders. The dead brother's counselor, who had treacherously made the murder possible, is brought to Vladimir's court, handsomely feasted, and made the recipient of prime honors for three days. Then said Vladimir: "I have fulfilled my promise. I have treated thee as my friend. Thy dignities exceed thy most sanguine wishes. To-day as judge I condemn the traitor and the assassin of his prince." And he slew him with his own hand.

His brother left a wife, a beautiful Greek nun, who had been captured on an expedition against Constantinople. Vladimir takes her also. Later he added four others, and had in addition in country seats and city palaces eight hundred concubines. Nestor calls him the Solomon of Russia—for his wisdom.

Ragneda, his first wife, forgave Vladimir the murder of her father and brothers, but complained at his infidelities. He therefore turned her out of his palace. One day in her lonely house he fell asleep, and she went in the room to kill him with a dagger. As she stole toward the bed he opened his eyes. "Put on thy wedding attire and await me in thy chiefest room," he said and his eyes spelled death. When he entered, their young son, in obedience to his mother's instructions, met him at the door with a drawn sword, saying: "Thou art not alone, father; thy son will be witness to thy deed." "Who thought to find thee here?" Vladimir said and threw down the sword. Quitting the place, he convoked his boyars and asked their advice. "Prince," they said, "spare the culprit for the sake of this child and give them for appanage that which was her father's." He did so and built a new city in it for them, naming it after the boy.

Vladimir's arms were invincible. He widened his conquests and cemented his empire. Expedition after expedition was successful. He drove back the pagan enemies swarming in from the east and built fortresses to keep them back. There are epic stories told about his campaigns. One day, embattled against the Petchenegi, they sent forth a hero and challenged one from Vladimir's army to meet him in single combat. When Vladimir looked at the pagan giant he despaired of finding anyone in his own ranks worthy to meet him and played for time. Finally an old man who already had four sons in the army came forward saying that he had a fifth son at home who was mightily powerful. He was sent for forthwith. A requirement to prove his prowess being laid upon him, a savage bull was brought forth and further infuriated with red-hot irons. The young man promptly engaged him, got his feet from under him, and, with what tactics I know not, reduced him to subjection, then with his hands tore off his skin as a trophy. The next day the Petchenegan giant laughed at the approach of the beardless youth, but the boy simply inclosed him in his arms and stifled him to death.

Vladimir himself came to be the center of a great cycle of legend. He was exalted above humanity and made the Sun God.

For all his victories he paid new honors to his gods. On one occasion he is said to have sacrificed nearly a thousand men. At another time the lot fell on a comely youth who was the son of a Christian. His father refused to give him up and repudiated the system that required such an enormity. Father and son were torn to pieces by the crowd, and the orgy of honoring pagan deities went on. New temples were erected, new images fashioned of gold and silver.

And now something happened which is explained variously. Some say that neighboring religions, seeing the enormous expenditures of Vladimir, desired him for their own, others that he began to realize that his pagan worship was not adequate either for himself or for his kingdom. Nestor says that of late he had been troubled much about the future life. However it came about, representatives of various religions came before him to present their forms of faith. Of the Jews he asked why it was that they had no country and that their disciples were wanderers upon the face of the earth. They replied that they had been so punished for their sins. He said he wanted no such religion. When the Mohammedans explained that wine was forbidden, but that their heaven was full of beautiful women, he asked why one indulgence was allowed and another prohibited. "And besides," he said, "no Russian can live without wine." He halted then between the Roman and the Greek Churches and sent ten learned men to make further investigation. They came back and reported that the Roman churches and service were bare and unimpressive and that the Roman pope claimed authority over monarchs. The Greek Church, on the contrary, offered freedom. What they had seen, moreover, at Constantinople left them awe-stricken. The glory of the Cathedral of St. Sophia, the splendor of sacerdotal robes, the magnificent imagery of the ceremonies, the presence of the emperor and his court, of the patriarch and processions of priests, the incense and the throbbing music sent them back north with the unqualified insistence that this was the religion for the Grand Prince and for Russia. "Further," they argued, "this was the faith of thy grandmother. If it had not been best, she, the wisest of mortals, would not have chosen it."

So Vladimir decides for the Greek Church. But how shall he be baptized? Not in any ordinary way surely.

He embarks an army on barges, dares the rapids of the Dnieper, descends to the Sea of Azov, and besieges Kherson in the Crimea. After six months a priest shot an arrow with a note tied to it telling of the spring in the hills that watered the city. Vladimir turned the spring, captured Kherson, and sent word to the emperor that he would have his sister in marriage or be in Contantinople immediately. The emperor promised, on condition that Vladimir would be baptized. Vladimir consented, and the weeping Anne was sent along.

When Vladimir returned to Kief he took back a train of priests as captives and loads of sacred ornaments and holy relics as booty.

He became now as zealous for Christianity as he had been in his old pagan faith. Perun, the father of the gods, he of the silver head and gold mustache, he had stripped of his ornaments, dragged through the streets at the tail of a horse, beaten by twelve men, and thrown into the river. Other gods suffered the same fate. Where pagan temples had been he built Christian churches. He called the people of Kief to the river bank and at signal, men, women, and children marched into the water while the priests standing with Vladimir read the baptismal service. He dismissed his many wives and concubines and was faithful to Anne. Like his father, he had eschewed beautiful things and kissed the sword. Not so now. Formerly Russian soldiers attacked churches and monasteries by preference, tortured monks and priests by driving nails through their heads and "sang them the mass of lances." He goes now to the opposite extreme, and the bishops have to remind him that enemies of the realm must not be suffered and that criminals must be punished. He distributed the public revenues to the poor in pious foundations and in great repasts in imitation of the love feasts of the primitive Christians. He was especially impressed with the two passages: "Blessed are the merciful" and "He that giveth to the poor lendeth to the Lord."

Vladimir, like all really great leaders, became a

patron of education and of art and applied himself to government. He founded schools where different classes in the community studied in the Slavonic tongue. Eminent teachers from Greece headed his educational movement. Records were encouraged. Artists and architects were brought from the south to build and adorn churches, palaces, and public institutions. Laws were softened and systematized and the land had peace.

All these reforms were greatly enhanced under his son, Yaroslav, but Vladimir laid their foundations.

Like many men of his day, Vladimir made the mistake of dividing up his realm among his sons, with no real bond of unity. With him even before his death it wrought tragedy. His eldest son refused to pay the small tribute required, and Vladimir sorrowfully gathered his army to march against him. He died of grief on the road.

That was A.D. 1015. He had reigned forty-five years.

By the nation he is given the title of The Great; by the Church he is sainted. In 1889 there was a great celebration of the nine hundredth anniversary of his conversion.

Looking at Vladimir and his country, one wonders about the effects of his choice of the Greek Church.

Russia thereby gained freedom from ecclesiastical interference, but it was loss as well. At certain stages of their development those old kings and governments needed the iron word of papal control. Europe fretted under it but may have profited by it. There are certain restraints which, in the last reaches of thought about them, are intolerable, and yet for the time are salutary.

Vladimir's choice of the Greek Church availed to separate his country from other countries of common origin, like Poland, and has given rise to a long series of tragic difficulties.

In like manner Russia was robbed of the Reformation and the Renaissance, which renewed Europe and spawned America. She became oriental rather than western, Asiatic rather than European. She has remained the child of Constantinople and has slept through the centuries. The Revolution of 1917 might have come two hundred years earlier or not at all.

Again looking at Vladimir and his country, we are reminded of the normal results of Christianity. There came in him and through him in his land a moral revolution. And that moral revolution was followed and accompanied by intellectual, artistic, economic, and industrial revolution.

Looking for a moment at his conversion and the reported circumstances, one is led to make a remark on beauty. The old story says that it was the beauty of the service at St. Sophia which captured him and his emissaries. I am interested in those old gnarled sons of the northern seas surrendering to beauty. Russia's achievements in beauty have since that day been far in advance of the ordinarily parallel lines of development. Her dramatists, her actors, her novelists, her musicians have held rank with those of any nation. Her music is to-day perhaps the most impressive on earth.

It is interesting that at this very time the concern most prominent in the mind of the Churches is to recapture a lost beauty for their worship.

The good, the true, and the beautiful—those are the three master passions of the human soul. Which comes first depends on the type of man we have. The prophet says goodness, the scientist truth, the artist beauty.

For myself I believe I would rather trust the artist in the quest of life than either of the others.

Beauty, it seems to me, is the earliest and the latest of the passions.

Let a man shake down the universe in his pan and the last particle that remains is the gold of love. The universe in its ultimate essence is kindly. Then let him take that particle and hold it up. It is beautiful.

But I must not forget that my general subject is Studies in Power. What shall I say? Power here is lost in mystery, as it always is really. Power rocked back and forth out there in Asia years and years agone. Then for a season of centuries power was transferred to a little country named Greece, and her sons went forth to conquer the world. In time the springs in Greece no longer bubbled, and Rome sat on her seven hills and swayed a scepter over all the nations of men. Then the ruddiness went out of Rome, and those crude Germanic tribes drove her armies and overran her palaces. Again the breeding ground of power is shifted. A strange race of men came out of the north. "The sea was their school of war and the storm their friend. They were sea wolves that lived on the pillage of the world." The day of power had dawned for the Vikings. Iceland was theirs; Greenland was theirs. They touched America. They threaded the pillars of Hercules.

They stabled their horses in Charlemagne's palaces and trampled his domain. They stood in Normandy and were looking at England. Denmark was theirs —Russia. And Vladimir was one of them.

What was the secret of that power in Asia, in Greece, in Rome, in Germany, in Scandinavia? No man knows. Even the causes of decadence are in the main veiled in mystery.

This is our day of power. When we fail, or if we fail, what will be the causes of our failure? And who will be next on the throne?

About the most that we can do in the midst of the mysterious shiftings of the seats of power is to realize that in the little day of each one of us there are certain great stern qualities that make for power, like honesty and courage and justice and patience and the faculty of seeing the invisible; and with reference to larger movements, so far as any opportunism is practicable, to observe if possible which way God is moving and try to move with him, as when Abraham came out of Ur, Moses out of Egypt, Paul out of Palestine, John Bradford out of England, Patrick Henry out of the old allegiance; as when any simplest man chooses not convenience but duty, not what he would like to do but what he ought to do.

WILLIAM THE CONQUEROR

ONE afternoon late we rode wheels into the old town of Bayeux in Normandy. We went leisurely about the cobbled streets looking for an interesting place to spend the night. Presently we came upon the interesting place, but as to whether we could spend the night there was another question. It was an old half-timber house on a corner. It looked as if it would just as soon fall down as not. Yet it gave one confidence, because if it had been going to fall it would have done so at least a hundred years back. The second story projected far out over the first, and the third just as far out over the second.

We looked at it with unalloyed delight and finally could not resist trying our luck. They took us in. In fact, later we discovered a very retiring announcement to the effect that guests were invited. The stairway went almost straight up about a central rounded timber. The room that we were given was precisely in keeping with the exterior; and the dining room as well, with its old furniture and silver and the excellent dinner that came later, served in quaint and formal style.

As we sat eating, sight-seers passed and looked in, and that night our guidebook told us to be sure and see the house at 145 Rue St. Martin, as it was five or six hundred years old. Looking for 145 Rue St. Martin, we found we were there.

The next day we examined the Bayeux Tapestry. It is some two hundred feet of linen about eighteen inches wide, with figures woven in wool. It is perfectly preserved, though possibly eight hundred and fifty years old. The story it tells is of William's invasion and conquest of England. They call it there Matilda's Tapestry, and it may be that William's queen wove it herself or with the assistance of her maids. Freeman, the great historian of the Conquest, regards it as the most trustworthy source of information that we have of the period and the achievement.

Then we rode on down to Caen. There we saw the great churches which William and Matilda built in expiation of their sin of consanguineous marriage. They were the greatest buildings of their day and, despite their immense age, are still in constant use. They are inspiring yet and architecturally are interesting even to a layman, as they show so plainly the beginnings of the arch in building, which in later

Gothic structures, as at Amiens and Chartres, is to leap and soar.

After Caen we took the beautifully shaded road and pedaled our way through the smiling fields of Normandy to Rouen, William's capital. Here, however, Richard the Lion-Heart and Joan of Arc crowded him out.

But back to Caen, and Falaise, the castle near, where William was born. It is now in ruins. In the year 1023, however, it was the ducal palace of Normandy. Young Robert was shortly to become the sixth duke in line from Rollo. One day, returning from an errand on his horse, he saw some girls washing clothes in a stream near the castle. They were laughing and talking together, apparently unmindful of the gay youngster riding by on his fine horse. One of them, however, caught his eye. On inquiry he found that she was Arletta, the daughter of the village tanner. Robert sent for her to come to the palace and live with him. Her father was uneasy, but a brother of his, who was a religious hermit, assured him that it was perfectly in order to do anything for so great a man as the Duke's son. So Arletta was decked out in her best and sent to the palace. She became the mother of William the Conqueror.

Not much was thought of such irregularity in those days. It had almost become regular in William's ancestry, but in this case some of the interesting and important developments of William's later life may have grown out of the circumstances of his birth.

For example, look at this picture: In the palace court a cavalcade of restless horses and of sumpter beasts ready for journey; within the palace an assembly of the important men of the Duchy of Normandy. At the head of the hall stands Duke Robert, taller and more nobly dressed than the others. His hand is on the head of a little boy five years old, and he is saying: "I go now. In my absence this is your Duke. If I do not return, the succession falls on him. Alan of Brittany here is his guardian." And Duke Robert, the father of William, the little boy, rides away and never comes back. Where was he going? On a pilgrimage to Jerusalem to see the Holy Sepulcher. He died in Greece. Such pilgrimages were not infrequent in those days for the fancied good of men's souls and the expiation of their sins. Robert's may not have had anything to do with William's birth, and yet it may.

But here is another picture, rather darker, that has a secure basis in that birth: In one of William's campaigns the city of Alencon was barricaded against him. As he came near the walls the defenders shouted insults about his birth and his grandfather the tanner. Finding that insufficient, they brought hides and hung them up and danced and shouted: "Hides for the tanner! Hides for the tanner!" William was so infuriated that he stormed the walls and captured thirty-eight men. He then cut off their arms and legs and, with the machines used for hurling stones, threw the ghastly pieces into the city. Again he dashed at the walls, entered the city, and drove the garrison into the citadel. He was tearing at this when the defenders offered to surrender on condition that their lives were spared.

Another much more important and more typical development came largely perhaps by reason of William's birth. His father was hardly gone before anarchy broke out. Those were pretty stern and lawless days, and pretty stern and lawless were those far sons of Rollo the Viking Northman, who had captured that country and called it Normandy. There might have been violence and insurrection under any boy. Those men needed the mailed fist in control.

But, at any rate, those who led the revolts, which almost immediately began, raised a sort of battle cry that they were unwilling to be governed by the illegitimate grandson of a tanner. King Henry of France, seeing his chance, aided and abetted the enemies of the boy Duke and invaded and harried Normandy himself more than once. William escaped every kind of death, eluded every kind of pursuit, evaded every kind of plot. Loyal friends stole him away at night and hid him in the homes of the poor, galloped across the country to apprize him of danger, died for him. William himself came to have the scent of the wolf for peril, the cunning of the fox in outwitting his foes, the endurance of the jackal, and slowly also the strength of the lion. It is probable that without those days of training he never could have been the conqueror of Britain.

William's father had said to those assembled noblemen, "He is little, but he will grow." And he grew. Slowly the boy gave place to the man. The green stick gave place to the bone, and the bone to iron. Slowly William conquered the place where he stood. He subdued his own land. He mastered Normandy. Guy of Burgundy was the backbone of opposition. Finally William met him at Val-es-dunes. William was nineteen, but much older in experience and power. It was a battle of horse against horse and man against man. Those were the days of personal encounter. "Here William began that career of personal success, of good fortune in the mere tug of battle which, till the clouded evening of his life, was as conspicuous as the higher triumphs of his military genius and his political craft. Men loved to tell how the young Duke slew Hardrez, the choicest warrior of Bayeux; how the veteran champion, in the pride of his might, rode defiant in the front rank; how the Duke rode straight at him, not jousting with his lance as in a mimic tourney, but smiting hand to hand with the sword. The poet rises to an almost Homeric flight when he tells us how William smote the rebel below the chin, how he drove the sharp steel between the throat and the chest, how the body fell beneath the stroke and the soul passed away."

Guy of Burgundy fled from Val-es-dunes, but William shut him up in his castle of Brionne and starved him into submission.

But William was not always the lion. He was more generally the fox. He wore the skin of the fox in patience and cunning, until the moment to strike, then changed to the other skin.

In his conquest of Maine the city of LeMans was the capital and the chief seat of resistance. It was strongly fortified and strongly held—an excellent opportunity for brilliant exploits and the waste of men. William did not use it so. With his army he went slowly about the surrounding country destroying the supplies upon which the fortress fed. Finally when he arrived at the gates surrender was ready.

Henry invaded Normandy in power. He had two armies. They ravaged the country everywhere and were carting off the wealth of the land. William said not a word. He waited. At last the army under Henry was crossing the river at Varaville. Henry with the head of the column was across, the body of his force heavy with booty was not yet over. William struck from the side, cut the army in two, and destroyed its rear, recapturing the spoils. Henry, from the heights on the other side, could see, but the tide was now coming in, and he could do nothing. Henry's other army was camped in the other part of the Duchy. William now sent to that camp a man who, in the night from some high rock or tree, called out with an eyrie voice: "Frenchmen, awake; you sleep too long. Go bury your friends dead at Mortemer." No more was necessary. The army beat a retreat to its own land.

And William was master not only of Normandy and more lately of Maine; but his over-lord, King of France, no longer dared trespass on Norman territory.

William's domestic life shines like a good deed in a naughty world. Perhaps partly for purposes of state he desired Matilda, daughter of the Duke of Flanders. But having won her, he loved her well and long.

A story is told of his courtship by Abbott and Guizot. Freeman does not mention it, evidently because he does not believe it. At any rate, the story goes that Matilda at first refused him on account of his birth. William, one day in her father's castle, is very rough with the lady, going so far as to drag her about the room. He then presses his suit again with her father. Her father as a form submits the matter to his daughter once more, and she at once accepts. He asks why, after refusing the first time. She replies that she had not known him so well before.

During all the years he is faithful to her and she to him. All the while he is in England she is the able occupant of his ducal dais in Normandy.

One of the most thrilling episodes in all the career of William occurred just as he was preparing to sail out of the mouth of the Somme for England. He had gathered his ships, some six hundred in number, from his various nobles. All sails were set, when from the south hove in sight a barque which, as she came closer, showed herself the gallantest of all the fleet. It was the Mora, Matilda's gift for the expedition. The Mora's wide sails were spread to the wind, and on the prow was a boy blowing an ivory horn which, when she swung around, pointed to England.

Nor is it without appropriateness and interest that the great Duke and his great Duchess, who were so lovely and pleasant in their lives, should have their magnificent memorials together, the churches that they built in Caen.

These churches stand not only as a sentimental symbol of the conjugal happiness of William and Matilda, but as a more direct symbol of their interest in the Church at large. William was genuinely a churchman. There was in his reign a revival of religion. He appointed good men to ecclesiastical positions. With his Viking gift for using talent wherever he found it, he invited men from many lands. There is a correspondence, for example, with the monks of

Sinai. He encouraged monasteries. It was not unusual in his day for wealthy men to found such institutions and then go into them as votaries. The most famous monastery in Normandy was Bec. It produced Lanfranc, who probably had more to do with William's life and achievement than any other person, with the possible exception of Matilda. In England William made him Archbishop of Canterbury. Bec produced Anselm, who formulated the theology still taught in many of our seminaries and preached in many of our churches.

William promulgated in his realm the remarkable Truce of God, as it was called. In a war-ridden age men were forbidden to fight, except in national crises, from Wednesday night till Monday morning, thus dedicating to peace the days of the week hallowed by the final sufferings of Jesus.

William's conquest of England added to his military renown, but did not enchance his reputation for moral idealism. He had visited England and said that Edward on the basis of a slight relationship had promised him the throne upon Edward's death. Later Harold visited Normandy and in his turn promised to support William's claim to England. Then Edward died. Harold was elected to the English kingship by the English Witan, or governing body. William had no right to the English throne, because it was not within the gift of either Edward or Harold or both. But he set about quietly to bring Christendom to his view. Slowly and with great craft he wrought upon the minds of men. Propaganda was not born in our day. Lanfranc even won the enthusiastic support of the pope for William's advance upon England. William's statesmanship nowhere more conspicuously appears than in his success in giving his invasion of England the guise of a holy war. One historian calls it the first crusade.

So here is his fleet with Matilda's ship leading, and yonder are the unprotected shores of England.

Strange upon what small events and combinations of events great issues hang. Harold knew about William's preparations and led an army to his southern shores. But William was detained by contrary winds, and Harold could not hold his temporary force together. When William finally sailed, Harold was up in the north at Stamford Bridge driving back another invader, the redoubtable Harold Hardrada from Norway. William, incidentally, may have fomented that other invasion to make his own easier. Harold had won a glorious victory at Stamford Bridge and was sitting at a banquet in the great hall at York when a courier rushed in to tell him that William had landed.

Back to London goes Harold, and down to Senlac, where what we know as the battle of Hastings was fought. Harold took his place on the crest of a slight rise, and William came on. The two greatest men in the world at that time faced each other. It was genius against genius, power against power. Often that day the English ax cleft rider and horse at one stroke. Often that day the Norman club felled rider and horse at one stroke. William finally won by the device of a pretended flight and by arrows shot up to fall in unprotected faces.

With transcendent ability William subdued and ruled England. He was hard, but perhaps a face less stern would have blanched at the supreme difficulties. He had himself regularly elected to the kingship, and there was no immediate change. Slowly, however, he surrounded himself with his own and gradually bent his kingdom to his will. England became Normanized. Norman blood became ascendant in English life. Many of the greatest English families and many of the greatest American families trace their lineage back to the Norman Conquest.

And with the stream of Norman blood came also the streams of Norman culture and the Norman tongue to enrich our speech and our life.

William's greatest single achievement, however, was in cementing England as one man to the throne. The mistake theretofore had been in the creation of proud earls, to whom the common man gave allegiance rather than to the king himself. William in his "Doomsday Book" set the whole kingdom before him, in personnel and in property, and on Salisbury field required the oath of allegiance from every man.

But as so often happens, a change for the worse appears in the Conqueror. He grows more ruthless. Too much power. Northumberland was hard to govern and he made it a desert. At least one execution cannot be defended. Nor can the formation of the New Forest with its inhuman game laws, blinding men for slaying the king's animals.

But compared with the men of his time, even in character, William was rightly called the Great. Among unchaste men he was chaste; among cruel men he was clement; among deceitful men he was direct; among strong men he was stronger still. Christian virtue begins to appear in William the Conqueror. We have here no appeal to superstitious fear as in

Attila; no enormity like human sacrifice as in Vladimir; no misunderstanding of the whole nature of God with reference to humanity as in Genghis Khan.

I shall but mention four qualities of power that were in him.

1. His capacity of using difficulties. Oliver, in his "Life of Hamilton," remarks of George Washington that he had enough difficulties to have slain any ordinary man, but instead he seemed to grow stronger by reason of them. It was so with William.

2. His finesse in battle and everywhere. He was not a mauler. He used the arts of the statesman. There are two ways of getting through a crowd, or handling children, or running a business. One is to fight your way through; the other is to bow your way through William employed the latter.

3. His not borrowing color from his surroundings, but giving color to them. He was independent. He was different. He was individual. He was himself. He was a flaming soul fusing the stuff of life and not a piece of putty molded by circumstances.

4. His undeterred continuance. He drove straight at the heart of the battle and would not be gainsaid. When others stopped he was just then beginning. When he was down it was only in order to rise again. When he was whipped he did not know it.

RICHARD THE LION-HEART

THOSE were the good old days.

They had gallant ships and swift steeds, but when Richard went on his Crusade it took him eleven months to reach the other end of the Mediterranean.

Good old days, but the arts of surgery and of consistent kindliness left something to be desired. Richard needed money to carry on his wars in France. He always needed money. And a peasant plowing in a field near Chalus had run into something, which on investigation proved to be valuable treasure. It is described as "an emperor with his wife, sons and daughters, all of pure gold, and seated around a golden table," and also some old coins. It was in Richard's realm, and a part of it was sent to him, but he wanted all of it. He laid siege to the castle of Chalus, whose ruined tower still stands on a hill above the river Tardoire. For three days Richard's miners dug under the walls while he rode about them with his crossbowmen discharging a shower of missiles into the inclosure. On the afternoon of the third day he ventured forth without defensive armor except a headpiece and a buckler. A man among the besieged had been nearly all day on a bastion of the tower with a frying pan in one hand and a cross-bow in the other. With his improvised shield he warded off arrows and with his weapon he was evidently trying to get a fair shot at Richard. When his opportunity came he had discharged all his quarrels, but snatching one of the enemy's from a crevice, where it had stuck in the wall, he hastily adjusted it and let it go at the king. Richard heard the arrow coming, looked up and shouted applause at the daring bowman. He ducked to shelter himself under his shield, but too late. The arrow struck him in the left shoulder. He gave orders for an assault and rode quietly to his tent. In trying to pull the arrow out he broke the shaft and left the point imbedded. A surgeon was sent for and then another, and the steel was finally removed with some difficulty, but blood poisoning set in, and he realized the end was near. The castle had been taken. He hanged its defenders, except the man who had wounded him. Of him he asked: "Why didst thou kill me?" The man replied: "Thou didst slay my father and my two brothers with thine own hand. Thou wouldst have slain me likewise. Take what vengeance thou wilt." Richard ordered him liberated with the gift of a hundred English shillings.

Those were the good old days. Men took the Cross, as the expression was, and wore the sacred emblem on the shoulder to signify that, as soon as circumstances allowed, they were going to Jerusalem to seek to wrest the Holy Sepulcher from the Infidel; but in Henry's time (Richard's father), the Cathari, a little irregular sect, were stripped to the waist, whipped, and turned loose to die.

Tournaments were held all over western Europe, and knights in shining armor and on caparisoned horses traveled far to balance their lances in the lists; but trial by combat was regularly used. If a man appealed or did not accept his guilt, he fought his opponent, and if he lost his battle he lost his case.

Those were the good old days.

The name of Christ was on many lips; and yet it is said that one hundred and twenty thousand men were buried outside Acre in a single year during the long attempt to retake that city from the Saracen armies.

Those were the good old days.

But on the 20th of August, 1190, after Acre had fallen under the thrilling attack of Richard, the Saracens were watching from a hill about two miles away. A little after midday they saw the great form of the English king come out on horseback into the middle of the plain with what looked to them like "the whole Frankish host." Moslem prisoners, who represented practically the whole captured garrison of Acre, were led out bound into the midst of the Christian army and put to death with swords and spears. Richard himself stated the number of the slain to be about two thousand six hundred. Bohadin, Saladin's secretary and companion, says above three thousand. Nobody apparently was disturbed by the wholesale murder. The chroniclers of the time all record it without hint of reprobation, one who was present going so far as to rejoice in the just vengeance that had fallen on the pagan for the Crusaders slain during the siege.

Those were the good old days when knighthood was in flower. But when Richard was raising money for his Crusade he taxed every man one-tenth of his movable property; the Jews were taxed one-fourth. At his coronation trouble arose with the Jews. It spread to many places and many were killed, although Richard, to do him justice, sought to stop it. Later, at York, five hundred of them with their wives and children went to the governor's palace for protection. The governor was called away and on his return was denied entrance. He gathered a force and attacked the palace. The Jews inside buried their gold and silver, cut the throats of their wives and children, and stabbed each other to death, rather than fall into the hands of our ancestors.

Those were the good old days. But when Richard's brother was dying and sent for his father, his father was afraid to go, thinking it might be a plot against his life. Richard's mother was kept in prison for a number of years by his father. Richard and his father and brothers were at actual war among themselves for years. Richard's affianced bride was intrusted to his father as guardian, and Richard himself with others accused his father of having used the girl for his own evil purposes. While Richard was away on his Crusade, his brother, John, raised the flag of rebellion and sought to tear his kingdom from him. Richard was recalled by that news and had to take the field against John upon his arrival in England.

Those were the good old days. But Richard and Philip, King of France, brother Crusaders, fought all over France, quarreled incessantly during that winter in Sicily on the way to the Holy Sepulcher, quarreled and finally broke completely as they faced Saladin, and continued to quarrel and fight after Richard's return, for Philip had returned apparently for the purpose of stealing Richard's holdings in Normandy and Aquitaine.

Our sympathies are with Richard—and yet those were the good old days.

Coming back from Palestine, Richard attempted an overland journey and near Vienna fell into the hands of the Emperor, who for personal reasons threw him into prison. Richard, in his various adventures, had fallen afoul of a number of the Emperor's friends and relatives and had to pay the price. While the homeland was trying to raise the amount of Richard's ransom, Philip, his brother in the Cross, and John, his brother by blood, were offering ever-enlarging sums to keep him in prison.

Those were surely the good old days.

The Crusades form the magnificent and amazing background of the life of Richard. That strange obsession spent itself in nine waves that rolled eastward to die or fall back from natural barriers or Saracen arms. Millions perished amid prodigies of valor and orgies of cruelty. Women dressed up in armor and marched to the Holy Land. In one pathetic slaughter of the innocents we are told that fifty thousand children perished in the sea or were sold into slavery.

Yet the Crusades had substantial results. The Crusades, the Reformation, and the French Revolution have been called the three great movements in the intellectual, economic, and political life of Europe.

The Crusades threw vast quantities of treasure into money and put it into circulation. So many thousands taking off from Italian ports laid the foundations for the city states, which later were to characterize that civilization. Feudalism began to lose its hold in the new political liberties that were born. Van Loon tells interestingly about the old barons borrowing money from the Lombard bankers to make the trip and then having to borrow again from their own villagers to make the payments. The villagers would lend, but would ask certain privileges in return, like the use of the baron's fishpond or his hunting preserve. Distribution of culture and of material comforts resulted, because the crude Westerners came into touch in the East with a much higher civilization than they had known before. And they met chivalrous foes there, much to their surprise and enlargement of vision.

Richard's early life was spent mainly in France, campaigning back and forth over the territory which he had inherited through his mother. Hundreds of the fortress castles of that day fell to his determination, his daring, his cunning, and his prowess. He fought his father and his brothers and then, with his father and brothers, the kings of France and lesser knights and counts who rose against him.

His Crusade cost him some two years. His imprisonment consumed another year. Then he was back in England and France for five years more before his death. He died at forty-two. He was in the middle thirties when in Palestine he was astonishing the world and capturing the imagination of time with his reckless daring and his feats at arms. But he had been at that for twenty years. His career at war really began at sixteen and a half years.

His Crusade Richard regarded as the most important achievement of his life. The "work of God" his contemporaries solemnly termed those serried marches upon the Holy Land. And when he tore himself away it was with the full determination to go back and complete it.

In the sculptured likenesses of Richard that remain the features are well proportioned and finely formed. He had a mop of hair "of a color midway between red and yellow." He was tall, shapely, and powerful. A born athlete, he adorned himself with the richest clothes, art assisting nature.

Richard is not the only hero whom French poetry declared possessed of a lion's heart, but he has kept the description and tied it to his name against the field and for all time.

Kate Norgate, Richard's latest biographer, quotes from Gerald of Wales, a contemporary chronicler: "Among the virtues in which he excels, three especially distinguish him beyond compare: Supereminent valor and daring; unbounded liberality and bountifulness; steadfast constancy in holding to his purpose and to his word." "Strictness and firmness, gravity and constancy," another of that day puts it. And still another: "In the list of the kings let there be written down the Duke of Aquitaine and Gascony, Richard, who has never been slack in deeds of prowess, and whose youth is distinguished by great strenuousness of life."

He was called in his day Richard Yea and Nay. Maurice Hewlett takes that to mean that he was a house divided against itself, that his mind and heart never really got together. It seems more probable that the name originally meant that he was a man of few words and of definite acts.

Women apparently played no part in the life of Richard the Lion-Heart. He married rather late Berengaria of Navarre, but was notoriously false to her. In fact, she seems to have meant very little to him. There was no great love in his life.

That is probably, in a large sense, the weakness of Richard. He had no great love. His life was without focus. He is a creature of his whims and bent about by circumstances. Magnificently gifted, he lent himself to occasional purposes here and there. He did not learn to subdue himself to some overmastering cause, therefore achieved no mighty or enduring ends. He was brilliant but not solid. He took forts, but he did not hold them. He was daring but not patient. He could dazzle the world, but he could not bend it slowly and permanently to his will. He is best known by his Crusade, and yet he loitered months on the way—fighting endlessly and without much aim, first in Cicily, then in the Island of Cypress, while the combatants impatiently awaited him at Acre.

Richard was at heart a troubadour with a battle-ax.

Romances sprang up everywhere about him. Robin Hood was in Sherwood Forest in Richard's time. And Blondel, so the story goes, went about Europe singing a song that he and Richard had sung together, till, finally under a prison wall, his first verse was answered with the second from within, and the royal prisoner was found.

So lived and died the mighty Richard.

As such a sun goes behind the horizon we may well reflect upon the necessity of great character having a great cause. The two are bound so closely together that some historians insist that men are not the makers of movements, but are made by them. That is not wholly true, I think, but it is undoubtedly true that three of the elements of greatness are the discernment to see the great cause, the courage to espouse it, and the constancy to live and die with it. This is also true, that many a comparatively small man is made great by loyalty to a great cause. That is the psychology underlying the politician's anxiety to get hold of an issue. That is one of the missions of college fraternities, of political parties, of the Church, of the family.

In the second place, looking back at Richard's time, we are led to reflect that one is very unwise who denies hope to backward peoples. England, the modern mother of civilizations, was in those days but little removed from barbarism. Yet after the expiration of these few centuries we see what we see. Indeed, so long ago as our national birth England was burgeoning with the fairest truths of civilization that the earth then showed. The genius of Christianity is faith in nations and in men when every outward mark seems to rebuke that faith.

But as we are not to be discouraged when nations and individuals are for the time being estopped of progress, neither are we to imagine that we ourselves or others, having begun to advance, must of necessity continue. Nations and men are able to dam up the ongoing streams.

There had been higher stages of advance than in Richard's day. There had been more stable government. There had been vastly superior civilization. There had been purer Christianity. But affairs had slipped backward. Luxury had crept in. Personal ambition had stormed the castle. Sleeping sentinels had allowed the enemy to creep up in the night. Faithless watchers had let the sacred fires go out. Some runner had not passed the torch along.

It is so in our day. Many of yesterday's greatest

civilizations are decadent now, or dust altogether. Many of our noblest cultures are overrun now with weeds. Many of our finest families must go to old annals or to forgotten graveyards to remind themselves and to convince others that they once were great. Nothing is commoner than to see hands empty of scepters they used to wield, heads bare of the crowns they used to wear.

"What I say unto you, I say unto all, Watch therefore."

GENGHIS KHAN

HE is riding at breakneck speed. His whip uncoils like a snake along the horse's heaving flank. Behind, to right, to left, before, is the illimitable stretch of the desert. The boy's face is set. He leans far forward. The village tents come into view. Before the one in the center, around which the others are clustered, he draws rein, swings off, and rushes in. Too late. His father is dead. "How? Why?" "Poisoned, we think," his mother said.

Already the mourners were lifting their voices in lamentation, and already the deserters were leaving. Why risk themselves to the protection of a boy? "The deep water is gone," they said, "the strong stone is broken. What have we to do with a woman and her children?"

Houlun, his mother, did what she could to stem the tide. Taking the standard of the nine yak tails, she rode after the deserters and persuaded some to turn back their herds and carts.

In the fertile and wooded lands to the north, where the nomads got all their living, Targoutai raised the flag of revolt and announced himself overlord. The boy went into the tent alone and wept a little, then came out and faced life. He was thirteen.

Targoutai was coming, was not far away. The boy fled. He took to the gorges and remained in hiding for days. But hunger drove him out. He was captured and led before Targoutai, who commanded that a *kang* be put upon him, a wooden yoke for the neck with the two wrists strapped to the ends. In the murk of the tent the boy brought down the *kang* upon the head of his keeper and escaped. He stood in the bushes at the edge of a river and watched his pursuers as they sought him. He noticed that one of them saw him, hesitated, and then went on. He left the river, followed the horsemen back to the camp, and then went to the tent of the man who had not betrayed him. The man split the *kang*, burned up the fragments, and hid the boy in a cart loaded with wool.

The others searched the tent for him. They thrust spears into the cart. One of them wounded him in the leg.

His friend gave him food and a bow with arrows. "The smoke of my house would have vanished and my fire would have died out forever if they had found thee," he said.

He found his hungry family in hiding with a poor string of eight horses. He visited the scattered members of his father's clan, of his clan now, demanding the tithe of animals due to him as khan. Then his horses were stolen.

He started out alone after them on his tired sorrel mare. For three days he followed the trail. The dried meat, which he carried between saddle and horse to soften and warm it, had given out, and the horse was tired. The fourth morning he came upon a boy of his own age milking a mare. The boy tied up his leather sack, hid it in the grass, caught fresh horses, and went with Temujin after the stolen property. They brought back the eight horses, after killing one of the thieves with a well-aimed arrow. They had been gone six days.

Back to the camp of Borchu's father, for Borchu was the name of the generous youth. They took in the sack of milk as they entered.

"When I saw him weary and anxious," Borchu explained, "I went with him."

The father was pleased. He had heard of the adventures of Temujin. "Ye are young," he said; "be ye friends and be ye faithful."

Temujin leaving, said to Borchu: "Without thee I could not have found and brought back these horses, so half of the eight are thine."

But Borchu shook his head. "If I should take what is thine from thee, how couldst thou call me comrade?"

They gave the young khan food, a bag of mare's milk, a gift of black fur for the family, and sent him on.

Temujin is growing in strength.

At seventeen he married.

He had been engaged for years, from before his father's death, but had not claimed his affianced bride till now. With his companions he rode to the tent village of the father of Bourtai.

"When I heard of the great enmity against thee, we did not look to see thee thus alive," he was told.

There are feasting and music and laughter. On the third day the bride sits on the left of her father, dressed in white felt with high and elaborate headdress, and everything is ready for the start of the journey to her husband's home. But away she has gone, darting in and out among the tents, the groom in swift pursuit. He goes through the ceremony of struggling with her sisters and maids and bears her finally in triumph to his horse.

And so home. But there was not much peace in the Gobi Desert in 1179. A fierce tribe comes down from the north, throwing blazing torches among the tents, and is off with Bourtai, the young bride. With the help of an old friend of his father's, whom he calls on now for the first time, Temujin falls upon the village of the raiders on a moonlight night.

"The scene is described in the chronicle—Temujin riding among the disordered tents, crying the name of his lost bride—Bourtai, hearing his voice, running forth to seize his rein and be recognized.

" 'I have found that which I sought,' the young Mongol called to his companions, dismounting from his horse."

There are many women, but only one Bourtai. Her intuition and decision saved him from many a plot. We come upon her weeping by his bedside: "If thine enemies destroy thy heroes, majestic as cedars, what will become of thy small weak children?"

Temujin's clan numbered thirteen thousand warriors. Moving down a valley from summer to winter pastures, he is attacked by the old enemy Targoutai with thirty thousand men. He formed his wagons, on which the tents rode, into a great hollow square. The cattle he drove into the square; into the wagons he hurried the women and the boys, who were armed with bows. Then he faced the thirty thousand with his thirteen thousand, divided them, and beat them.

Temujin is growing. He is gathering paladins about him, known as the Raging Torrents. Borchu is among them, the boy of the fresh horse and the bag of mare's milk, and Chepé Noyon, the Arrow Prince, and Subotai, the Valiant.

Chepé Noyon, a youthful member of a hostile clan, was surrounded by Temujin and his Mongols. "Give me a horse," he said, "and I will fight any man among you." Temujin gave him a swift, white-nosed horse, and he cut his way out. Later he returned and said he wished to serve Temujin.

"Long afterwards, when Chepé Noyon was ranging through the T'ian Shan, hunting down Gutchluk of Black Cathay, he gathered a drove of a thousand white-nosed horses and sent it to the khan as a gift and a token that he had not forgotten."

Subotai was prudent, of grim purpose, and dared all things for the young khan.

"I will ward off thy foes," Subotai said to his master, "as felt protects from the wind."

"I was like a sleeping man when ye came to me," Temujin said to his heroes. "I was sitting in sadness aforetime and ye roused me."

The Mongols were still one of the weaker peoples of the Gobi, but a hundred thousand tents now followed the standard of the nine yak tails.

Temujin was thirty years of age. His sons rode by his side.

And a determination was forming in his mind.

"Our elders have always told us," he said one day to his council, "that different hearts and minds cannot be in one body. But this I intend to bring about. I shall extend my authority over my neighbors."

As if sensing his designs, the desert clans united against him, drawing in even Moghrul, his father's old friend. They had decided that he must be exterminated and came on in numbers to make it a fact. All day the battle raged. Temujin was sore pressed. At dusk he called one of his sworn brothers, Guildar, the standard keeper, and ordered him to circle the enemy to a hill called Gupta on their left rear.

"O khan, my brother," said Guildar, "I will mount my best horse and break through all who oppose me. I will plant thy yak-tailed standard on Gupta. I will show thee my valor, and if I fall, do thou nourish and rear my children."

It was the favorite strategem of the Mongols by which they turned the enemy's flank and took him in the rear—the circling standard sweep. It saved that field for Temujin and his clan, and legend still tells the story of how Guildar bore the nine yak tails to Gupta.

That was a desperate day, and little save a remnant was rescued, but Temujin's determination had not suffered.

"Couriers were sent to the near-by clans, and soon the khans of his own domain and their neighbors were kneeling on either side of the white horse skin of the Mongol chieftain, their feet tucked under them decorously, their long coats bound with ornamented girdles, their lined, bronzed faces peering through the smoke of the yurt fire. The council of the khans."

The bolder spirits prevailed for carrying the war forward and Temujin was given the leadership.

In a great battle the confederacy was broken. Old Moghrul was slain and his skull set in silver by the officer who achieved his death.

Wealth was now coming to Temujin—"saddles covered with colored silk and soft red leather, the thin and finely tempered sabers, the plates and goblets of silver, tents hung with cloth of gold," and settled cities.

And men. He had needed men. Now they were coming.

He knew how to bind them to him. Surrounding the residue of a vanquished clan, he offered them their lives. "Men fighting as ye have done to save your lord are heroes. Be ye among mine and serve me."

And he knew how to cut them off out of the land of the living. His cousin, Chamuka the Cunning, was made captive and brought to him.

"What fate dost thou expect?" Temujin asked.

"The same that I would have bestowed upon thee had I taken thee," Chamuka responded. "The slow death."

He referred to the dismemberment that begins the first day with cutting off the first joints of the little fingers and continues up all the limbs. Instead, however, he sent him away to be strangled with a silk bowstring or stifled between heavy felts, according to the custom of the Mongols which forbids spilling the blood of a chieftain.

And he knew how to adopt new things. A captive was seen clutching a gold object.

"What is that?" Temujin asked.

"My lord marked his orders with this seal to show they were in reality royal commands."

Temujin ordered one made for himself of green jade.

Captured astrologers and physicians became his servants.

His horsemen were now ranging from the sea to the valleys of the western Turks.

Again he calls a council of the khans, this time to choose a single ruler for upper Asia.

The choice fell upon Temujin. A soothsayer arose to suggest a title, Genghis Kha Khan, the Greatest of Rulers, the Emperor of All Men.

Genghis Khan promulgates the Yassa, his code of laws, and lays an organization upon his even farther stretching domains. The Yassa, says Harold Lamb, to whom I am chiefly indebted for all I have been saying, the Yassa aimed at three things: obedience to Genghis Khan, a binding together of the nomad clans, and the merciless punishment of wrongdoing. The organization of his fighting force, which was really the organization of his clan, was like that of the Romans.

And now his eyes turn toward Cathay—China. There was wealth there and an ancient civilization. He needed both. Wonders were told about Cathay. Men wore nankeen and silks of many colors there, the roads ran right on over rivers, wooden wagons floated on the rivers, cities had walls. Instead of old minstrels, young poets sang for royalty, and they sang about the beauty of women. And his men needed war. Peace abroad meant war at home. "He meant to harness the whirlwind and direct it away from the Gobi."

He said to them: "These men who will share with me the good and bad of the future, whose loyalty will be like the clear rock crystal—I wish them to be called Mongols. Above everything that breathes on earth I wish them to be raised to power."

With his grim determination he began to penetrate beyond the Great Wall.

Slowly he brought to submission the Golden Emperor, he and his sons and Chepé Noyon and Subotai and Muhuli.

But no luxurious South for Genghis Khan. Back to the Black Sands, with Muhuli at Yenking in charge of the new empire.

But he was not through. He said to his sons one day, "The merit of any action is to take it to its end."

In the pavilion at his desert capital he asked an officer what could bring the greatest happiness.

"The open steppe, a clear day, and a swift horse under you, and a falcon on your wrist to start up hares," the officer said.

"Nay," responded the khan, "to crush your enemies, to see them fall at your feet—to take their horses and goods and hear the lamentation of their women. That is best."

His eyes are now in the west. He opens trade with Islam—the Islam of Arabia and Persia and Syria and Hungary and Russia. Some of his envoys are killed, and his armies are soon on the move. They were some two hundred thousand strong and had hitherto impassable mountains to cross and millions to face on the other side of them.

In a sentence we must freeze and starve with them and then gallop with them over thousands of miles as they leveled scores of cities, slaughtered millions of men, and chased their enemies over dozens of countries. They trampled under foot Bagdad, Damascus, Samarkand, Bokhara, Kiev, and Moscow. And in the midst of it the khan called them to council two thousand miles to the east, and they galloped back. The whole thing is unparalleled in history, and one of its minor movements has been called the greatest achievement in the annals of cavalry.

Genghis Khan is back at his desert capital, an old man now, but moves against the Sung Dynasty in Southern China. On the way death overtakes him. He goes into his tent, appoints his successor, and dies. It is important that his enemies shall not know of his death, and as they drive the body back everybody that sees the funeral cortège is killed.

Genghis Khan's empire did not break up at his death, as has been so often the case. A generation after he was gone the Mongol horsemen were riding over Western Europe, and all Christendom was in consternation. Carpini, Rubruk, and Marco Polo all visited Cathay during the time of his grandsons. And the empire had grown, not shrunk. Marco Polo tells of Kubla Khan's curfew, his police regulations, his giant system of restoring lost articles, the thousand carriages of raw silk per day entering his capital, his magnificent summer and winter palaces, his trained leopards, lynxes, eagles, and lions for hunting, his masters of the chase with ten thousand men each, with their contract for one thousand pieces of game per day for the royal table, the khan's own ten thousand falconers for his personal hunting and ten thousand watchers of the game, his ten thousand post houses and two hundred thousand post horses covering their two hundred to two hundred fifty miles a day, the one hundred thousand horses that came on every birthday, the one hundred most beautiful young women gathered annually for his harem.

Genghis Khan was called in his day the Mighty Manslayer, the Scourge of God, the Master of Thrones and Crowns.

Probably nobody who has ever lived can compare with him for sheer power. His contemporaries explained him as an emissary of Satan, as Antichrist, as the incarnation of the force of barbarism, as the instrument of God to punish nations for their sins. But to this day he remains unexplained and unexplainable.

Massive results followed his conquests, such as the diffusion of the knowledge tied up in Western Asia in centers like Bagdad, such as the limitations set upon Mohammedanism, such as the unification of the world of that day, such as the driving of Turkey into Europe, such as the opening of India.

Looking at the career of Genghis Khan, we are reminded of that well-nigh universal law that conquest is by the ruder, more primitive peoples. The finer civilizations go down before the barbarians. Alexander, walking up and down in the conquered cities of Asia, is amazed at their luxury. Rome in turn topples over the priceless art treasures of Greece. Again the Germanic tribes profane the temples and palaces of imperial Rome. The Vikings come on the stage and once more the savage is tearing down silken hangings and scoffing at the more delicate achievements of culture. And in obedience to the law, Genghis Khan, son of the Black Sands, unlettered Mongol, gallops with his paladins over the finest civilizations of his world.

Looking at our own nation, we ask ourselves if there is any way to avoid the fires of cleansing which history has invoked ever so often for the civilizations of the past. Is there any way to become cultured without becoming effeminate? Is there any way to amass wealth without inviting in the hurricanes of wrath? Is there any way to keep beauty and power wed? Can our experiment of freedom in government and religion find a way to survive? Is there enough of moral challenge in our Christianity, and are we presenting that phase of it with enough insistence to keep us alive? Or is our religion becoming just another one of those easy methods of dying that the other great cultures of the world have found?

Again, looking at the Master of Thrones and Crowns, one reflects that with him and his people Christianity missed an opportunity of the ages.

The Jews missed their chance with Alexander the Great. He was not very far from them. If they could have composed their own affairs and flung themselves out with their revelation of God, only so far as Macedonia, they might have changed the face of the world. Paul got there four hundred years late. Genghis Khan was religious after his fashion. The first provision of his Code of Laws, his Yassa, was that men should believe only in the one true God. But he did not know the God and Father of Jesus Christ. There were Christians in his realm, but they were of a sect who spent their strength in theological distinctions instead of purveying the life of

God to men. When the matter is broached by Marco Polo to Kubla Khan, he is interested and asks that the pope send one hundred learned men to teach him and his people the true nature of Christianity. It is never done.

Are we presenting a type of Christianity that appeals to the weak and flabby and leaves to one side the masters of men?

Finally, as we reflect on the power that Genghis Khan developed over on the other side of the world from his small beginning in the Gobi Desert, we ask ourselves, Where has that power gone, and will it come again? One of the theses of modern thought is that nothing is lost. Of course it has been scattered in portions all over the world, but doesn't the bulk of it sleep over there waiting to rise again and play a new rôle in the life of men? Are those seers of the race right who look across the Pacific and say that the next act of the great drama of humanity will be played in the Orient? And if the Orient does come back, if Genghis Khan does live again in his far descendants, with what mind will he come? Will it be Christ or Antichrist, to slay or to make alive?

It behooves us to do all we can in our little day

and in our little way to make the world one, that when history's new sons of power arise it will not be nation against nation, but the undivided earth against the prince of darkness, of ignorance, of superstition, of confusion and division.

JOAN OF ARC

JOAN OF ARC is one of the remarkable appearances in human history. Outwardly Paris in many of its aspects is a brilliant memorial to Napoleon, but the heart of France still marches behind the Maid of Domremy. Many of the monuments which commemorate the Emperor were erected by himself or brought in as booty from other countries. His pictures are still prized, his institutions still used, his laws still obeyed, his annals of victory still recited. She took no booty, founded no institutions, wrote no laws, wore no crown, but in times of national crisis it is the spirit of Joan of Arc that is invoked, not of Napoleon Bonaparte. Hers was a spiritual conquest, which grows not less but greater with the increasing years and with the increasing appreciation of the sources and nature of power.

Her bare story is romantic beyond belief.

Other women have taken the sword, but they were titled ladies with retainers and ready-made armies to call into action and with the long habit of authority and the custom of kings and queens. Joan was a peasant. They were of mature wisdom and command. Joan was a girl of seventeen. They held single castles or fought single engagements. Joan fought whole campaigns. Circumstances flung them into the military leadership which they assumed. Joan made her own circumstances.

Other mystics have heard the voice of God, like Socrates and Paul and Francis of Assisi and Teresa. But they were led to shaded walks for teaching or to preaching campaigns, or to hermit cells for meditation and prayer. She was led to the company of kings and to the command of armies. They were men and women, she a girl; but she assumes men's clothes, buckles on armor, mounts a war-horse, and, waving her sword, advances to the attack, saying: "Onward, my comrades; God will give us victory."

Yet we are not to think of her as ethereal. She was intensely practical, hard-headed, full of common sense. She was no wraith, but robust and hard-handed. She laid about her with right good will in many a battle. The picture of her in the Metropolitan Museum in New York has her too old, it would seem, but the semblance of physical vigor and resourcefulness is probably true to life. She was not peculiar in that time for hearing spiritual voices;

she was peculiar in strength and endurance and courage and initiative and leadership and patriotism and unselfishness.

Nor by her mission was she rapt away from woman's nature. She cried a little on occasions when she was wounded, though wounds did not keep her from the saddle and the forefront of battle. Her explanations on trial as to her reasons for wearing men's clothes were essentially those of a shrinking country maiden; and her answers to many questions were typical of a bright, clever, precocious, even pert, girl.

A thousand legends grew up about Joan even in her day. There is a theory that it takes time for such growth. Her case and our own experience prove the reverse. These legends were in two streams, one critical and scurrilous, the other laudatory and romantic. That is always true. Every public servant, no matter how heroic, has a swarm of detractors who go about repeating things that are purely legendary. We must expect that. On the other hand, every public servant, no matter how unheroic, has a swarm of admirers who go about repeating things that are purely legendary. These two streams struggle for supremacy. In most cases, the cynics to the contrary notwithstanding, if a man is really heroic and successful, the positive wins; if he is really unheroic, especially if he is unsuccessful as well, the negative wins. But there are always legends. A man is either worse than he is or better than he is, depending on which direction he is going. A good deed is frequently worth ten times its apparent value because it starts a whole air-full of echoes. Let a man be brave, resourceful, successful, and legends envelop him so that he is scarcely visible. His legends take arms and fight for him. That is not a sufficient reason for good deeds. Control of legends is political manipulation. But if a man misbehaves and finds in circulation all sorts of stories that exaggerate his misbehavior, let him not complain. That is the way with legends.

After all the only brave and righteous way to conduct life is to go on with it and let legends take care of themselves. The English and Burgundians said that Joan was a witch and a shameless woman following soldiers about. They so shouted to her from many walled cities that she approached. The play of Henry VI, supposed to have been at least retouched by Shakespeare, accepts that traditional English attitude. But none of these things moved Joan.

She went her way. She did her work. To the simple country people and her friends among the French she was the special representative of God; she was irresistible; she was divinely instructed in statecraft and generalship; she foretold the future; she located Charlemagne's sword; she had miraculous power over animals; she prayed the dead alive; her banner was sent to her out of heaven; men saw armed knights riding through the sky prefiguring her victories. Nor did these things move her. She did her best in a very-matter-of-fact, common-sense way to deny them and set the truth to the fore. She never traded on legends. She was willing to abide by facts, and facts there are in plenty. Mark Twain, in the preface of his romantic biography of Joan, says that she is peculiar among mortals in having every fact of her life attested in court and under oath. He is referring, of course, to her trial which preceded her death and to the investigation which preceded her reinstatement by the Church twenty-five years later. A full report of the trial and reinstatement, published by Quicherat in 1841, brought the whole subject of Joan's career out of the fogs of medieval fancy into the clear light of plain record. She was found to be a simple, strong, vivid, faithful, pious, chaste, country girl, who heard the Voice of God and did what she could to obey it.

So she stands at the last, as all of us must stand, unhurt and unhelped by legend.

Just to the rear of the cathedral in Rouen is the archbishop's castle. On its outer wall is this inscription: "At this place in 1456 Joan of Arc was rehabilitated by the Church." She was rehabilitated as a good Catholic, and yet in reality she was not a good Catholic, certainly not in that day; for she was never willing to say that she would intrust to the Church the question as to whether her voices revealed to her the will of God. She insisted on the right of private judgment. In every other particular she was perfectly orthodox, but there she was a heretic of the heretics. A very interesting thing in this connection is a letter which she signed, though she is not thought to have dictated it, to the followers of John Huss in Bohemia. She calls them heretics and enemies of the Church and threatens to march against them and either convert or destroy them. John Huss was one of the early voices of the Protestant Reformation, one of those who died a short fifteen years before for their faith that the individual stands immediately before God without the necessary mediation of the Church.

Joan and John, whether they knew it or not, might have shaken hands from their funeral pyres, for they were kindred spirits, seeing alike that the individual soul is free. As Shaw says, the law of God is the law of change. And the only way that change can be effected is to free the individual to hear and see for himself.

Joan received fair enough treatment when everything is considered. She was surrounded by the Burgundians and pulled off her horse by her brilliant cloak at the hands of a soldier. She was sold to the English, as the rules of war in that day permitted. She was turned over to the Church for trial as a witch. That was in accord with custom and in accord with belief at that time. She could have escaped death by throwing herself into the arms of the Church and letting it decide upon the validity of her voices. That she refused to do. And there the old and the new came into conflict, the orthodox and the heterodox, the organization and the individual. It was an inescapable struggle, and some individuals had to die to win it. Joan was one of them. She is one of those casualties of progress which make all true history tragic.

When Joan was thirteen she began to see her saints

and hear her voices. Anatole France with great care and prodigious scholarship makes it all very natural. He explains how she came to realize the depredations of the English; how large a part in the worship about her and in her national heraldry St. Margaret, St. Catherine, and St. Michael played; how she was familiar with an old prophecy that a virgin should free France; how priests coached her; how soldiers used her. But the facts remain that she had to win her way against soldiers in the first instance and later to drag them to attack and to victory on more than one occasion when they had voted quiescence or accepted defeat; that she first saw her mission before any priests could have thought of coaching her; that any other girl of her time could have realized the need just as vividly as she did and had the identical likelihood of hearing divine voices impelling her to meet it. No, she was a genius in insight, in decision, and in action. The ordinary explanations do not apply in her case. We have to realize that some people are, as William James, I believe, calls them, visualizers. Intuitions are delivered to them visually. It is Bernard Shaw who says: "If Newton's imagination had been of the same vividly dramatic kind, he might have seen the ghost of Pythagoras walk into the garden and explain why the apples were falling."

The test of such intuitions is not how they come, but what they do after they come. The method may be unusual, even grotesque, but that is beside the point if the result is practical. She became convinced that she could and ought to drive out her country's enemies. And she did. Nobody doubts that the method she chose was wise—that of raising the siege of Orleans and leading the dauphin to Rheims to be crowned. That was good policy, and she did it. Her visions were leading her truly.

In like manner, on the basis of evidence given in her trial, there have been interesting findings about an avowed physical abnormality in Joan. It is shown, to the satisfaction of some, that she never matured as a woman, and that that great surge of physical being, as imperious as the multitudinous feet of posterity, failing a natural outlet, chooses an unnatural—sees disembodied faces, hears disembodied voices, and finally leads dispirited armies back to victory. That may be true. It is certainly interesting. It is also certainly unimportant. The question is not what method God uses, but whether God is using it. And the way to determine is by the outcome. By their fruits ye shall know them applies to visions as well as to persons.

But her voices failed? Yes, that is true. Cowardice, treachery, personal ambition, unwillingness, imbecility were too much for her. She tried to hurl the king and his council against Paris, and they would not go. Half-supported, she was driven back. And that was the beginning of the end. They sent her here and yonder to get rid of her, and she could but fail again. She was captured and thrown into prison and tried and done to death, and they raised not a hand in her behalf. Her voices failed? Yes and no. In 1431 she was burned in Rouen. In nineteen years, of all their great holdings in France, one little spot, Calais, remained to the English. In nineteen years a new trial of Joan of Arc was begun, which ended in a retraction of her conviction, a public procession, and in the Old Market, the place in which "the said Joan was cruelly and horribly burned to death," were decreed a solemn discourse and the erection of a decent cross to keep her in everlasting remembrance. Nineteen years. Too late for Joan, but not too late for the vindication of right and the progress of the world.

Goethe is right in his address to her:

"Up, up, the earth flies back!
Brief is the pain, eternal is the joy."

There are two things for us to remember about the Voice of God: We are not to doubt its validity in the experience of others because it comes in an unusual way, and we are not to doubt its validity in our own experience because it does not come in an unusual way. God speaks to all of us if we will hear.

An enormous lot of difficulty and lost motion and failure could be obviated if we approached our problems and our burdens and our battles as Joan of Arc did. Of course she was a genius and we are ordinary people. We cannot be sure as she was. But we could at least approach our lives from above. If we believe that there is a Divine Spirit in the universe which can hold converse with our spirits, we ought to manifest it more definitely by living in accord with it more truly. If we even believe that there is a concrete totality of environment and of being, an assembled wisdom and strength of the universe and of time, we ought to seek to know it and to live in unison with it. It is a very simple sort of thing—this ignorant girl out in the garden, hearing voices, and finally against many difficulties making her way to the king to lay her plan before him. But surely that is the type of thing we all ought to be doing. No man of us really believes that he lives alone. We all have our voices. The trouble is we do not listen attentively, we do not cultivate them, we do not launch upon the adventures to which they challenge us. Somebody asks an explanation of our conduct, or inquires delicately about the basis of our lives; and we turn away or give some noncommittal answer, when what we needed to give and what they wanted to hear was an affirmation of our voices. Thus we weaken ourselves and thus we fail in leadership. Joan this way accomplished the impossible. She convinced many people that she was moving at the behest of God. She did not push herself forward; she would accept no praise. There was no self-consciousness in her and no personal ambition. "Our Lord," she insisted, made the plan and carried it forward. We are bound to admit that here we have run upon one of the primary sources of power. "What are angels, prophets, men, but pipes, through which the breath of God blows a momentary music?"

Now Joan sealed all of this and seated herself forever upon her indestructible throne by dying.

Before the scaffold a sign was placed on which was written for the instruction of the multitude:

"Joan, who has taken the name of the Maid, liar, wrongdoer, deceiver of the people, witch, superstitious, blasphemer of God, presumptuous, unbeliever, braggart, idolater, cruel, lewd, sorceress, apostate, schismatic, and heretic." The scaffold itself, on which the wood was piled, had been made high, so that all the crowd might see the burning. As Joan was about to mount it with her confessor, she asked for a cross. An English soldier gave her one made on the spot from two sticks fastened together; she kissed it devoutly and, praying all the time, thrust it into her bosom under her dress. From the church of St. Saviour opposite they brought her the crucifix, and this, too, she kissed and embraced while they bound her to the stake.

After the fastening had been secured, the executioner set the fagots afire. The scaffold was so high that he was hindered in his work, and the wood did not burn as quickly as he had expected. When Joan saw the flame, she told La Pierre to descend with the crucifix, and she begged him when he had done so to hold it up for her to look on as long as she could see. She had not lost her faith in her voices, or else it came back to her in the fire, for those standing near by heard her speak the name of St. Michael, who had appeared to her in her first vision in Domremy. At the last, through the flames, they heard her call again and again with a loud voice, "Jesus, Jesus."

She held the mirror up to Christ in an unusual way. There was no real fault in her, brave to the point of recklessness, true to the point of suffering, seeking not her own, and at the end paying for it all with death.

We live in a strange world, and there is nothing stranger in it than the power of guiltless sacrifice. The greatest of the Hebrew prophets, that unknown Second Isaiah, saw it long before Christ: "He hath laid on him the iniquity of us all. . . . Therefore will I divide him a portion with the great." Paul saw it long before it began to work itself in history: "He humbled himself to death, even the death of the cross; wherefore God hath highly exalted him, and given him a name that is above every name." George Washington saw it and Lincoln and Lee. Lenin knew it. The greatest word ever written about it is in this clause: "The lamb slain from the foundation of the world." The principle is operative universally and eternally.

PHILIP II OF SPAIN

It was in the royal palace at Valladolid. The year was 1527, the day was the 21st of May, and the clock stood at four in the afternoon. A woman said to those in attendance: "Put a cloth over my face that not even an involuntary wince may be seen." They remonstrated, but she said, "No, die I may, but wail I will not." For she thought she was bearing the Emperor of the earth. And she was. She was the mother of Philip II.

That day or a day or two thereafter there was a bullfight in the public square. The victim was dispatched quite handsomely by the greatest toreador that ever thrust home the fatal sword between the shoulders of a bull. It was Charles V, Emperor of Rome, Emperor of Germany, King of Belgium, the Netherlands, Spain, parts of France, Italy, Asia, Africa, and half of the New World. It was the father of Philip II. He was celebrating the birth of a son.

The people were wild with joy.

So was ushered in the frail child, who was to inherit the greatest empire of that time and in some respects the greatest empire of all time. He was slight, preternaturally grave, of delicate pink skin, of yellow silken hair.

When he was hardly more than a boy the arrangement was made for him to marry Mary of Portugal. He had never seen her and was not supposed to see her until properly presented. But as she came on to the Spanish capital he rode out with some companions and met her, and under the disguise of a silk mask played along the way with her and her group of attendants.

But that summer-time of his spirit was of short duration. The gloom of his palace and of his family and of his responsibilities and of his disposition soon encompassed him altogether. He came of epileptics. Two of his brothers died with it and a number of his ancestors. His family were religious mystics with strange notions about God and duty. His mother died early. His first wife had already died—he was a widower at eighteen. While still young he married Bloody Mary, who was ideally fashioned to contribute any gloom that he might have lacked and to encourage those qualities in him that were most productive of gloom. As a child he probably heard thousands of prayers for the success of his father against the heretics and came to see himself in his imagination already carrying forward that holy war.

1. Philip was from the beginning and increasingly self-centered.

He thought he loved Spain, and he did. But he loved Spain because Spain was himself and her exaltation meant his.

He thought he was religious, and he was, deeply so. But he saw himself as the patron and protector of the Church and the exalted arbiter of all religious matters everywhere. His various marriages were political and religious in purpose. One is to cement relations with Portugal, another to combine with England against France, another to combine with France against England, another to safeguard eastern possessions with Austria's aid, and all to unite the forces of Catholicism against the encroachments of Protestantism, or what was known then as heresy. Particularly was the marriage with Mary of England, "Bloody Mary," for the purpose of saving the day for the orthodox faith. Through the whole pathetic business Philip poses as martyr for Spain and the Church. But one feels vaguely that he is not only looking at himself in a mirror while he poses, but that he is prefiguring coldly the personal advantages that are to accrue. He comes slowly into the distant haughty magnificence of the Castilian manner and to the superiority of a self-appointed savior of the world. He could not hurry, and he could not play. There was nobody to play with, and life was too serious, anyway. And why hurry? He and time were in league. His very patience was a sort of insult to the rest of the world.

He was very fond of his father and deferred to him in everything. His father lays down certain principles of government, and Philip asks no better than to follow them. His father wants him to marry Mary of England, and he writes that he is not interested, but is a dutiful son and will find pleasure in obeying. But always he seems to be enamored of the picture of himself obeying and reaping the consequent rewards.

2. Philip lived in the past. To him the future simply did not exist. He could see nothing except the same old method of taxing his realm beyond endurance. He was apparently blind to the fact that his father's system was already resulting in debt, in abandoned farms and factories, in discouraged artisans and rebellious subjects. Those things had al-

ways been so. What other way was there to conduct the government? Offices and political privileges had always been sold. Necessities had always been taxed, and luxuries had always gone free. The poor had always been ground underfoot; the rich had always been favored. The assemblies had always been dismissed as soon as they voted what money they could and before their grievances were heard. Promises to them had always been broken. They had always been told, "Well, we shall see."

His father had said to him: "Advance nobody. Play off men of ability against each other. Appoint men of opposing types as your councilors, not that you may hear all sides—you already know what you are going to do—but that nobody may be advanced except yourself. Do everything. Be everything." That was the way it had been and must, of course, continue to be.

In like manner there could be no possible change in the Church. It had always dictated the minutiæ of men's faith. It had always been supreme in its realm. It had always sustained a certain relationship to the state.

Of course no one of these things was entirely true. It was the immediate past into which Philip was looking. It was the immediate past according to which he was molding the present and all possible futures.

3. Philip slept on in the midst of the Great Awakening. The sun arose, and he never found it out.

He married Mary of England to add another throne to his dominions and to make England Catholic again after the rebellion of her father, Henry VIII, against the pope. He was twenty-seven; she was thirty-nine, and she fell passionately in love with her handsome, slight, dignified, patrician Spanish prince, of the blue eyes, flaxen hair, correct beard, and rich clothes. When after a short while he realized that she was going to die, disappointed of her pathetic, palpitant expectations of an heir, which she had recurrently and persistently cherished, he left England. Mary died without him, and Elizabeth came out of her prison and to the throne. Then he began to try to marry Elizabeth. Elizabeth played him as a cat does a mouse, as an angler does a fish that is below the legal limit and is to be thrown back even when caught. She dangled him in the air. She kept him alternately hot and cold. She invented other suitors that made him jealous and other alliances that made him afraid. She may not have known her own mind always, but he never knew it at all. He was not a fighter, but prided himself on his diplomacy. Elizabeth took him on his own ground and outwitted him at every point. But he never waked up.

In war she beat him as well. He finally realized that he would have to fight. Elizabeth's privateers were preying upon his treasure ships, and her soldiers were furnishing aid and comfort to his Protestant enemies in the Netherlands. He would have to fight. And the Great Armada sailed. The ships were of an old pattern and unwieldy, the water was stale and short, the food rotten, the discipline lax, the tactics of grappling and boarding archaic. Elizabeth's fleet was ready. With swifter ships and long range guns she sailed around and pecked away the life of the great flotilla. Storms did the rest. Expected reenforcements did not arrive. Out of one hundred and thirty ships that left harbor, sixty-five limped back.

Philip sat in the Escorial, the enormous palace he had built among the hills, symbolic of his self-esteem, his spirit of isolation, and his gloomy piety—Philip sat in the Escorial, among his papers, his figures, his details, details, details, pulling strings, as he thought, that reached all over the world. Philip sat in the Escorial and never waked up.

He finally sent the grim Duke Alva into the Netherlands to subdue that nest of Protestantism. Every footprint of Alva's in that unhappy country oozed with blood. He executed upwards of eighteen thousand people, besides the thousands more whom he drove out or imprisoned or froze or starved. On one occasion, when a number were making secret plans to move away, he executed five hundred of them. He invented new types of torture. He bled the country not only of its people by his cruelty, but of its resources by his senseless taxation. Then William the Silent arose. Alva destroyed his army. William raised another. Alva crushed that one. William raised still another. He retired into the waste places, into the flooded areas. He organized secret forces and fought on land. He organized the Beggars of the Sea and fought on water. Philip and Alva were two of a kind—patient. But they had met another more patient than themselves. They could defeat him and his people, they could destroy them, but they could not subdue them. But Philip never waked up.

Philip slept on through the Great Awakening.

New liberties were being born everywhere, and Philip never became aware of it. It was not the great leaders in Spain who were complaining about taxation, methods of government, and invasion of popular rights. It was the people. It was not kings who were defying him in the Netherlands. It was the people. He learned very definitely in England that Mary could not have her way; he learned that he could not succeed her. He saw the terms of the contract of their marriage dictated by regularly chosen representatives of the people. He complained with members of his suite, who were with him in England, that monarchs in that country had no real authority.

And as he strangely did not see the sovereign people arising to assume the scepter of government, neither did he see the influences which were causing them to rise. He did not realize that the great classics, including the Bible, were being made accessible to all men and that a marvelous new ferment was at work in the soul of the world. He did not hear the religious reformers of his day pronouncing the everlasting principle of the equality of men before God, upon which all our modern government is supposed to rest and upon which all government must ultimately rest. To us, after these centuries, those voices seem to thunder; but Philip slept on.

Philip was a patron of the sciences, yet Copernicus, Tycho Brahe, Galileo, and Bruno were stretching above him a new heaven, and he did not see it.

Philip was a patron of literature, but Cervantes and Shakespeare both lived and wrote in his day, and he did not realize that they portended new things. Don Quixote went off in the same room with him, and he did not wake up.

Philip was a patron of art, but he lived in the same world at the same time with Cellini, Leonardo, Michelangelo, Raphael, and Velasquez and did not realize that anything strange was happening. Titian painted his portrait without arousing him.

Philip lived in the midst of the most important religious period since the days of Jesus and the Apostles, without any apparent consciousness of the fact at all. He was contemporary with Luther, Melanchthon, Erasmus, Calvin, Zwingle, and Knox, and gave no sign of his awareness except to go patiently on, trying to root out the new freedom in men's thinking about God.

The Inquisition was his instrument. The very word is still a-shuddering among men. During its process 31,912 were killed in Spain alone; 291,450 were imprisoned and tortured. During its brief operation in England in Mary's time, three hundred were burned, among whom were the great names Cranmer, Latimer, Ridley. One day in his capital city Philip sat on a raised platform watching the victims go by for the burning. An old man, whose limbs were all twisted from the torture and who was going now to his death, appealed to Philip: "Why have you done this?" Philip answered: "If my own son were as obstinate as you, I myself would bring the fuel to burn him." He had a number secretly murdered and sought the same means of taking off for Elizabeth of England and thought that he was doing God service. It has even been said that Philip was behind the massacre of St. Bartholomew, when 100,000 of the best blood in France were lost by death and flight. The very language of the Inquisition afflicts us even at this distance with a sort of dumb terror. "Mother Church" extended "tender mercies" to the soul by disciplining the body. When the accused escaped death and was to be imprisoned, it was spoken of as "reconciliation." When the verdict was death by burning, it was called "relaxation." And Philip sat in the gloomy Escorial pulling those strings, all unaware that the sun had risen.

But let nobody imagine that Protestants were very much wiser when their turn came. Calvin burned Servetus at the stake because his views of the Trinity were not regular, and senseless religious persecution was even transported to the shores of America. Catholicism wanted to make the world safe for Catholicism. Protestantism for Protestantism. Neither was wise enough, nor are we to-day, to realize that the world must be made safe for humanity and freedom. Maryland, by the way, a Catholic colony, was the first in this country to declare for full religious liberty.

It takes time. Not everything at once. However, the sun was rising, and Philip drew the shades with those delicate fingers and slept on.

There he is in his great gloomy pile, with his silken beard, his self-esteem, his sense of duty, his details and his strings. The crack of doom had come, so far as he and he régime were concerned, and he knew nothing about it. In every department of life men were splitting the sky in two. In Philip's day Columbus had just made the greatest discovery of the ages, as the event proved, and Captain John Smith and Governor Bradford were trembling on the lip of the greatest colonization enterprise since the world started. Philip's own men were ranging the earth for adventure and gold. DeSoto is in Florida; where Augusta, Ga., now stands; hits the Mississippi near the site of Memphis; wanders around in Arkansas.

Ponce de Leon is down at Tampa Bay. Pinera is at Mobile Bay. Coronado is looking, the first white man, down into the Grand Canyon. Cortez is in Mexico. Pizarro is in Peru. Balboa is gazing at the Pacific. Magellan is circumnavigating the globe. It was even the golden age of piracy, for it was all in the game. Whole shiploads of gold and silver were plying from Mexico and Peru to Spain, and British privateers like Drake and Frobisher were chasing them over half the world. And Philip was still asleep.

So he sleeps on while his empire slips away, and Britain edges him out of the way and takes his place in the seats of the mighty.

Two remarks in as many sentences: It is possible for us as individuals and as a nation to sleep through the day of opportunity, and it is enormously important to understand the nature of God. The God and Father of our Lord Jesus Christ was not the God whom Philip served.

GEORGE WASHINGTON—
BENJAMIN FRANKLIN

The Period of the Revolution

George Washington.—American union is one of the impossibles of history. It could not be done, but was. Winning independence was miracle enough, but cementing it after it was won was much more. The Colonies were split a dozen ways. Some wanted three confederacies—New England, the Middle States, the South. What is now Tennessee and Kentucky formed another geographical unit. The mountains and the seaboard were counterposed, and the agricultural and manufacturing. Some were in favor of going back to the Mother Country. Some thought that freedom meant no government at all, some that any government meant a return to some form of monarchy. There were many ideas, but they all conflicted, and small irreconcilable groups clung to each. Meanwhile England, France, and Spain hemmed us in on all sides and waited for their shares of the splintered fragments that the inevitable explosion would fling them. It was simply an impossible situation. Yet out of it came order, union, and the beginning of what we know as the United States—the miracle of the United States.

Through those stressful days walks a man named George Washington. He was in the forefront of things—Commander in Chief of the Armies, President of the Constitutional Convention, first President of the Republic—and the wayfaring man, though not necessarily very learned, came to regard him as the Worker of the Miracle. Recently, however, a group of sad, wise men have arisen to tell us that Washington was really nobody and did nothing, or that whatever he did he did with his tongue in his cheek. This brotherhood of the finders of the cloven hoof, having convinced themselves that nothing is really worth while, set out firmly to drive us enthusiasts and gullibles away from wreathing fond altars to the memory of nonentities and self-seekers. But more recently still other adventurers into the farther facts, other microscopists and weighers of minute things, have brought back the word that all is well with the fame of Washington. "The monument still stands." And the sum total is good; he ceases to be a frozen paragon of abstract virtues and becomes a human being to be known and loved, but is nevertheless great.

John Corbin, in his very recent book, "The Unknown Washington," draws for us an exquisite picture of the romance of Washington and Sally Fairfax, and all the more exquisite because rigorously historical.

First, he is able to present us his hero cleansed of the vicious stains of political and war-time propaganda, which have so long clung to him, even in the minds of reputable biographers. Then enter George Washington and Sally Fairfax. She is the new mistress of Belvoir, eighteen-year-old bride of George Fairfax. Belvoir is the Fairfax home, five miles down the Potomac from Mount Vernon and in plain view.

In 1811 she died in England, and among her possessions were found two letters from Washington, which show beyond reasonable doubt that he fell passionately in love with her. The evidence is the more conclusive when taken in conjunction with entries in his diary and with other letters both of his and hers recently published. The whole picture, however, reveals the light, skillful fencing of a stainless woman and the iron resolve of a stainless man.

The incident is significant in Washington's career because it reveals a quality in him little accounted.

In the first of the two letters he writes: " . . . There is a Destiny which has control of our actions, not to be resisted by the strongest efforts of Human Nature." He was far from marble. There was human nature in him, but there was also destiny. He was St. George, but with his foot on the dragon's neck—and the dragon was never fully dead. Strong men fight to win their calm, and the fight is sometimes going on when they seem calmest. The story comes down of a battle between the boy Washington and his mother's prize stallion. The battle was not ended until the horse fell dead. It is a parable. The young Washington is born of wind and flame, but by slow degrees the elements of rebellion come under the mastery of his will. The young man, fighting in the wilderness, fighting the Indian, fighting the authorities for better organization and supplies, fighting Braddock for a method of advance, fighting for the rank of American officers, fighting for the Virginia route to Pittsburgh against the Pennsylvania, is not the George Washington known to fame. In those early years he resigned from the army seven times.

We are told these days that self-control is apt to be dangerous in the development of character. In opposition I instance George Washington. And until these modern apostles of anarchy in the personal life show me superior achievements, I shall go on preferring him.

The episode with Sally Fairfax has been called the most beautiful love story in the world. Certainly there are in it elements of unfading appeal—young passion, pathetic renunciation, wistfulness, silence, power. There came his one volcanic avowal—volcanic though restrained—possibly that the years of intimacy between the two families might proceed on a basis of truth. Then silence. On her part silence throughout—the silence that wise women know. Silence?—not quite; for she kept the letters fifty-three years. And who shall say her nay? It is no small thing to be loved by a strong good man, even though unhappily, and if that man later came to be the hero of the world, the reflection that she had had some part in the making of him and had swayed his great heart certainly would not take away from the sweetness of the memory. Silence?—not quite; for he spoke again. When he was sixty-six, just nineteen months before he died, he wrote once more suggesting that she come back to Virginia, and there "close the sublunary scene," and recalling the days that he had spent with her, "the happiest of my life." Martha wrote with him, adding her urgency and telling the news. I think she knew his secret. In the first letter and in the last one he uses the expression, "Time, that faithful expositor of all things."

Time. George Washington knew how to wait. He came but slowly into his own, but avoided the peril of the short cut. Impatience was to him weakness. Haste was betrayal of the soul. He knew instinctively that sudden forced growth is a promise without fulfillment and a deadly pitfall to him who invokes it or expects anything from it.

Time and silence. He was not a talker, but a doer. His arguments were acts. He did not record the inner movements of his mind. Years after his memorable winter there, visiting Valley Forge, he writes down the fact, nothing more, and then goes on to relate that he met a farmer who gave him some new ideas about corn. His careful diaries kept through many years do not discuss men or measures or events, though they were written when his world was in turmoil and epochal things were happening all about. He did not analyze; he exemplified. He did not debate; he waited and worked. Instinctive himself, he moved along instinctive lines in dealing with others, employing time and silence and deeds.

There are battles and battles. Not only on bloody fields, but in ladies' chambers and in winter quarters and in halls of council.

We have been considering one fought in a lady's chamber—after a manner of speaking. Another, fought in winter quarters against cold, hunger, sickness, and discouragement, was at Valley Forge. The Revolution was probably won there. Another finally came to drawn forces at Newburgh in March, 1783, and more than the Revolution was won there.

The war was really over, and Washington with his army was waiting for formal peace at his headquarters at Newburgh, N. Y. The war was over and won, but all would have been lost but for Washington's victory in the new building at Newburgh that fifteenth day of March, 1783. Years after, David Cobb, who was there, wrote: "I have ever considered that the United States are indebted for their republican form of government solely to the firm and determined republicanism of General Washington at that time." General Schuyler, wise and devoted patriot, wrote: "Never, through all the war, did his Excellency achieve a greater victory than this. The whole assembly was in tears at the conclusion of his address. I rode with General Knox to his headquarters in absolute silence because of the solemn impression on our minds."

The war was over, but the army had not been paid, Congress was impotent, chaos was in men's minds, mutiny was about. And much more than mutiny. The idea had been gradually forming that the only way out was for the army to take charge and force through some kind of order. Some of the strongest men in the country were behind the plan—a dictator was necessary, a king—and the army with its grievance was a ready instrument. If Washington was willing to lead, well; if not, then Gates. And many preferred Gates, including Gates.

The anonymous call had gone forth, and the assembly was met. Washington read his address, standing his six feet three inches and still an athlete despite his fifty-one years and his labors known to all. His uniform of buff and blue was, as always, immaculate. Yet things were not as they had been. He would have called himself now an old man; his hair was graying and his eyes dimming, and those before him, men of his own household, were his enemies, cold and resolute.

Yet he went on: "Let me conjure you in the name of our common country, as you value your own sacred honor, as you respect the rights of humanity, and as you regard the military and national character of America, to express your utmost horror and detestation of the man who wishes, under any specious pretences, to overturn the liberties of our country and who wickedly attempts to open the flood-gates of civil discord and deluge our rising empire in blood."

He read his own bold writing without difficulty, but when he began a letter, promising some hope from Congress, he found his eyes unequal to the task. Reaching for his glasses, just arrived from Philadelphia, he said simply: "You have seen me grow gray in your service. Now I am growing blind."

He read the letter and withdrew. The meeting adopted five resolutions rejecting with scorn the "infamous propositions."

Mr. Corbin suggests that David Rittenhouse and his spectacles may have saved the country that day. He also suggests, plausibly as ingeniously, that Newburgh was a logical sequence to Belvoir.

Belvoir, where Destiny and Human Nature were embattled; Belvoir, where, in the company of old Lord Fairfax and of his patrician daughter-in-law, Washington may easily have acquired his later manner and received his inspiration toward the things of the mind; Belvoir, where the Fairfaxes cherished their liberal passion, generations old, and whither Sally brought her additional flame of republican desire and devotion; Belvoir, where Washington may first have caught his vision of the America that was to be; Belvoir, where he first heard of "Cato."

They played Addison's "Cato" at Belvoir. Sally played Marcia. And Washington wrote that he would have been doubly pleased to take the part of Juba—the barbarian Juba against her patrician Marcia.

Just the light fall of a rose petal, yet years after he is iterating and reiterating words from Addison's "Cato":

> "'Tis not in mortals to command success,
> But we'll do more, Sempronius—we'll deserve it."

In the dark hours of the Revolution Washington repeated those words in his heart and wrote and rewrote to his comrades that, though they might not command success, they could still deserve it. At Valley Forge he had "Cato" performed and attended it with Martha.

But the more definite connection with Newburgh was Cato's refusal to follow Cæsar in leading the army against the republic. No denial of Cæsar's greatness, but Cato falls on his own sword rather than use Cæsar's method, even though it meant sharing Cæsar's glory.

So Washington still knows how to wait. He still trusts "Time, that faithful expositor of all things." Silence is yet his coadjutor, patience the man of his council. Destiny must still control Human Nature. And he has extended the principle: government is sacred; the individual must submit himself to corporate control.

And a further extension is this: the ultimate rightness and sureness of that corporate control. The people finally will do right. They are to be trusted. Washington's confidence that republican government was possible and that the American people could and would achieve it is one of the sublime things of history. He saw as those about him did not see. Imagination was, after all, the biggest thing in him—faith, the evidence of things not seen, the substance of things hoped for—faith in Destiny and his people.

Finally—a long, slow, painful finally—finally the Colonies met in a Constitutional Convention to arrive if possible—though few thought it possible—at some plan of union. Washington was there and president of the convention. He was there *silently* and having waited until *time* had made the people *feel* their need of union, for, he said, they will not *see* the need until they *feel* it. As a soldier representing divided Colonies, as an explorer of the West and owner of lands there, as leader of a revolution waged by a confederation, which was "no more than a rope of sand," he had long experienced the need of union. Since retirement he had sat little under his "own vine and fig tree," but had begun with deeds to make the Colonies *feel* their need of union, pressing his great plan of a waterway communication through the mountains to the West. And now Shay's Rebellion had come to accentuate the need.

And the convention was in session. Adams, Hamilton, Madison, Gouverneur Morris, Pinckney, Franklin carried the day for the Constitution. But wise men felt then and wise men feel now that the moral force behind the movement and the power of guidance in the movement was George Washington.

There is no more grateful picture of Washington—in the background, silent, letting others achieve the brilliant victory, willing to compromise in minor particulars, yet seeing the great central need and drawing all men to it, by force of character, by loyalty to the public good, and by fidelity to his enthralling vision of the future of the American people.

And he continued his sway over that brilliant coterie. If Beveridge is right in saying that the Virginia contingent was the greatest group of men ever brought together at one time and place, what shall be said of them when we add Pinckney and Rutledge from South Carolina, Franklin from Pennsylvania, Hamilton from New York, Adams from Massachusetts? Yet at their center sits Washington, dominating them all—not an intellectual man, not a highly educated man, not an eloquent man, not an agile or resourceful or bright or spectacular man—a simple, direct, practical man, meeting the great needs of his great day among his great associates with purity of aim, singleness of purpose, clearness of vision, and unapproachable glory.

BENJAMIN FRANKLIN.—Light-Horse Harry Lee said of George Washington what others have found easy to repeat: "First in war, first in peace, first in the hearts of his countrymen." Those are formidable firsts and perhaps unequaled firsts, but for variety and number Benjamin Franklin has an array that far outreaches them. The American Philosophical

Society, the American library system, paving, street cleaning, fire companies, commercial advertising, fertilization are among Franklin's firsts. He was the first type maker in America and the first ink maker. He made America's first copper-plate press. He founded the University of Pennsylvania, improved lamps, invented a stove, bifocal spectacles, and river chevaux-de-frise. With Dr. Bond he established our first hospital. Owen Wister says that he established the first Masonic Lodge, but Fay disputes that, saying that he got into one of the first Lodges with some nice contriving. Guedalla calls him the first American efficiency expert, the first American humorist, and, by reason of his activities with the Junto and his general attitude of helpfulness, certainly the first Rotarian. He was our first student of ocean currents and our first experimenter and inventor in electricity. He suggested daylight saving time. He devised a new kind of wheel, improved the harmonica, made observations of balloon flights, and discovered a remedy for smoky chimneys. He introduced new trees and new cereals. Russell describes him as the first civilized American, because he was first to conceive of God as interested in our pleasure. He was the first American diplomat—and the last, many say.

His friends claim for him the first plan of American union, but that can hardly be made out. He certainly was the first American to add to the world's list of literary masterpieces, where his "Autobiography" still holds place. Fay calls him the first bourgeois, the first common man to take position among the grandees of the earth. McDonald writes of him as the world's first great citizen.

Benjamin Franklin educated a nation and financed a revolution. Those two achievements raise him to the first rank of men.

Franklin's "Poor Richard's Almanac" became the handbook of American thought and life. Writing men are commonly accredited with the fatherhood of nations—Homer of Greece, Vergil of Rome, Dante of Italy, Goethe of Germany, Shakespeare of England. These men made the languages and opened the fountains of parent ideas, by which peoples have become one and have lived. Franklin suffers in the comparison, but he did the same sort of thing. He made a nation of efficient, practical-minded people. The fact is recorded with sorrow by the purist, and there is point to his contention. Franklin bent the tree, when it was a sapling, and inclined us to this day of money-making. We were the easiest victims in the world to the industrialism that came later. In fact, he himself was the first of the great industrialists and made it a cult. Honesty with him was a policy; virtue was commercial. The modern man, who asserts that consideration for employees is good business, ought to add, "As old Ben Franklin would have said." Of course it is good business, but it is vastly more. And it is in that vastly more that Franklin somewhat failed us in our novitiate as a nation.

However, what he did, he did incomparably. His sentences glance and cut now just as they did then. It has been asserted, and with justice, that he is not only the first of American humorists, but the father of American humor. He is no pale beginning, but the ebullient spring giving volume and character to the whole stream.

And what he did, he did to meet a particular need. It may be argued that the greatest need of his day was identically what he gave—prescription for honesty, economy, frugality, industry. His skill lay not only in preparing the medicine so that the patient took it all and called for more, but in divining just what was indicated, as the physicians say, in the particular circumstances. Certainly many people at that moment needed terribly to learn how to work and how to save. The world was coming into the new management of common mortals. They were building a new country, new liberties were about, with perils as well as satisfactions—all conditions calling for Franklin's homely medicine. It might be mentioned also that some other parts of the world might have profited at that time, and later, by some of the same simple and fundamental treatment. Again it might be mentioned that we as a nation would have fared better if we had earlier and more fully applied Franklin's doctrines to the matter of our natural resources.

Chiefly, however, it must be recorded in Franklin's behalf that, if he taught only practical things, he turned those practical things to high and spiritual ends. Human helpfulness was his purpose of living. He never worked alone, but always with and for others. He was indefatigably public spirited. Philosophical reflection, scientific experiment, artistic endeavor—all were bent directly to making life happier and fuller for his fellow mortals. Urged to take out patents on inventions, he refused, saying that he was not inventing for profit, but for the service he could render. He retired from business at forty-three for the purpose of securing "leisure, . . . for philosophical studies and amusements," but practically adopted from that time the profession of citizen. His retirement plan was ideally generous: David Hall, his foreman, was to pay him "one-half of the present profits" of the business for eighteen years, then become absolute and sole proprietor. As a boy he had read Cotton Mather's "Essays to Do Good," and it entered into his soul and informed him till he died.

Thus theory and practice must be taken together in any appraisal of Benjamin Franklin. He says to us in modern America: "The practical and the mechanical are inevitable. The machine is here. You cannot destroy it, and it is vain to hide your face from it. You cannot go back; you cannot go around. You must go through. The machine and all other exemplifications of the ever-present practical must be made to serve the higher ends of life. The purpose to which a thing is put determines its character."

And Franklin financed a revolution—the Revolution. Washington would have been powerless without him. Nor was it one of those formalities that anybody could have handled. Franklin was the only

American at all available for the task. No other was known out of the country. They were all young, in the first place, as compared with Franklin, and, however prominent they were later, they were not then even names. Further, Franklin had the advantage of five years' residence in England as the representative of the Colonies. But, more especially, his writings were known everywhere, for Poor Richard was almost as much a vogue in Europe as here. And, more especially still, Franklin was regarded at that time as one of the world's leading scientists. He was the Edison of the Revolutionary period. And much more, of course. For Franklin was not only a scientist and a patriarch, but a philosopher, a writer, a wit, a patriot, and the incarnation of the thrilling new republicanism just then coming to birth on America's golden shores. His arrival ran a titillation all over Europe, and France rejoiced as if a king were coming. A recent French biographer insists that Franklin could not have achieved what he did in France without his Masonic affiliation. The foremost Frenchmen were Masons, including even Voltaire and the King. And nobody knew better than Franklin how to employ that powerful influence. Nor did Franklin make the mistake of Frederick the Great in imagining that women had no part in government. Franklin taught even the French new finesse in the art of enjoying and pleasing the ladies. He rightfully estimated those subtle powers which intelligent and beautiful women exert upon the public and official mind. Indeed, the whole social world of France did obeisance to the simple Franklin. He came upon the stage at just the right moment. France was tired of the opulence and artificial grandeur which the Louises had shed upon the court and Paris, and Franklin, instead of aping the life he found, refreshed it with a draft of youth and nature. He was seventy years old, but young as ever, and he was out of the young West and unspoiled as the wind blowing across corn.

But, more than all these, Franklin was a born diplomat and one of the most charming men that ever lived. He knew France's natural interest in the Colonies, and for ten years he lived there with the French people, understanding them and drawing them to his cause. But even so he performed the impossible. He got millions of francs out of France's empty coffers. He got recognition and a treaty and an army and a navy. They could not resist his wisdom, his courage, his patience, his courtesy, his quaintness, his loyalty.

But let no man think that all of this was accomplished without the customary crucifixion. Republics are proverbially ungrateful—because republics are made up of human beings. Humanity has an interesting habit of acclaiming its heroes too early, then of turning and rending them to even the count, lastly of canonizing them after they are dead. Those who expect gratitude for benefits conferred are yet children. Franklin loved the Mother Country, living in London five heavy years, fighting the break with the Colonies; and the picture of Wedderburn and the Privy Council pouring scorn upon the old scholar's head is one that intelligent Englishmen do not like to recall. No more do sensitive Americans like to recall the Philadelphia mob stoning his house because things were not going well in England, or the conduct of his associates in France, impugning his motives, poisoning public opinion against him, and bringing Congress within an ace of recalling him. He suffered on and smiled on and worked on.

Humor was with Franklin a lifelong invaluable tool. Lincoln had the comic spirit, but it was paired with melancholy, and he came to be lonely and burdened almost beyond bearing. Lee and Washington had humor in the early years, but the weight of affairs crushed it out. Franklin was dowered with it as with a divine gift, and he kept it until the end—or it kept him.

Humor is edged, but, rightly used, saves many a shock of battle, with consequent loss or even defeat. It is a surprise action which captures without bloodshed, a feint which uncovers the coveted position, a flying flank movement which obviates the frontal attack. Nay, humor is the word and the glance which the day before battle renders battle unnecessary. It is the smile which often puts swords back in their scabbards. Humor is a magic essence which dissolves our ancient reserve and brings us together, kindred spirits in the bond of common blood. It is a flash of light revealing the face of brothers in the dark. Franklin had it—rich, true, multifarious, inexhaustible—and used it marvelously. Pretty broad sometimes, like cheese with a bite to it, quite shocking to puritanical and staid Philadelphians and Bostonians, but they always came back for more. And so did the world. And so has it ever since.

Franklin was no plaster cast saint. There are a good many things that we might find to regret in him. But he saved himself to genius and the ages by a passion of unselfishness. The impurities in him were never allowed to settle because the crucible of his life was always white hot. Everything he had and was he threw into the crusade to make men freer and the world better. He drowned the negative in a tidal wave of positive. What otherwise would have become débris was borne along with the spring freshet and added terror and beauty to its crest. But it is a mistake to speak of Franklin in terms of enthusiasm. He burned too quietly, he flowed too gently, he fought too slyly. He was too wise and calm and philosophic and quizzical and deft. He was too much of an empire builder to be a mere crusader.

He asked of God virtue, knowledge, a chance to help and an after life. I hope to meet him some day when we have all been corrected and amended. The famous epitaph by himself is:

THE BODY

OF

BEJAMIN FRANKLIN, PRINTER

(LIKE THE COVER OF AN OLD BOOK,

ITS CONTENTS TORN OUT,

AND STRIPPED OF ITS LETTERING AND GILDING),

LIES HERE, FOOD FOR WORMS.

YET THE WORK ITSELF SHALL NOT BE LOST,

FOR IT WILL, AS HE BELIEVED, APPEAR ONCE MORE,

IN A NEW

AND MORE BEAUTIFUL EDITION,

CORRECTED AND AMENDED

BY

THE AUTHOR.

ABRAHAM LINCOLN—ROBERT E. LEE

THE PERIOD OF THE CIVIL WAR

ABRAHAM LINCOLN.—"Live much in the open, associate with your superiors, and touch elbows every day with the common people." But there must be no faintest intimation of looking down when we say "common people." We are all common, else we are on the way to become common indeed, for humanity has a way of excising that which imagines itself superior. Proud flesh is rotten flesh. Everybody ought to take Walt Whitman for annual spring tonic to set the blood tingling once more with the passion of identification with everything human.

That is the trouble with ancestors. They beguile us into exclusiveness. Pride of birth may be a good thing, but it usually isn't. We follow the trickle and forget the river.

Education renders the same tragic disservice in many cases—or rather what we call education. It is academic. It leads away from life instead of into life. It roots in the air, being ashamed of the soil. It has no sense of continuity, no long, deep, wondering experience of growth into the fiber, into the blood of all that has been and is and is to be.

So all privilege is full of peril. It tends to break the connection, and presently we are without power and asking why; or, worse still, we are, like Samson, not aware that the Spirit of the Lord has departed from us.

Abraham Lincoln had no ancestors and no education, and when privilege came later it did not avail to lift up his heart and make him forget. He did not need to seek the common people every day. He never left them.

No poetry can blink the fact that Lincoln was born amid slatternly poverty or that his boyhood, youth, and young manhood partook of the obscenity and low things that we still think of as belonging to his class, but try to forget when our minds dwell on him. But Lincoln would not have been Lincoln had he not mirrored the life which surrounded him. Nor did he ever get away from that life. Until the last, enemies and friends alike saw in him the old crudeness of clinging soil. He never got away from that life. His roots were still sunk in it and, like great yearning arms, embraced and loved it all. He never got away from it, but he left it nevertheless. His world grew and he grew with it. The plain widened, but, his head always lifting, he saw it all and lived in it all—an old gnarled tree, roots deep sunk, and one with the mysteries of the soil, but later the strong shaft upraised, branches reaching out into another world, leaves spread in other mysteries of communion. Another world and yet the same. Just bigger and wider and richer, and Lincoln lived in it all and was part and parcel of it. One of the great politicians of all time, men say, the explanation being simply that he knew and trusted the people, being one of them. He knew what they thought because he thought it with them, and he had confidence in their ultimate honesty and justice because he had those qualities and he was no better than they.

Here stands Lincoln then. He knew what the people wanted and what they were willing to do to get it, and he stands in his day representing them and making claims on their behalf. He lived in them and for them. And this is a reason that he is become one of the sons of power, one of the timeless.

Lincoln had good judgment. Intelligence is a part of original equipment, but it is susceptible of cultivation. Lincoln was born with it, but he used it and added to it every step of the way.

It is a mistake to think of brain power as having to do with the higher mysteries of abstruse knowledge. The chief use of brain power is in making the ordinary decisions of life. Good judgment, common sense, is the highest glory of intelligence and a prevailing talisman in achievement. Just to be able to go along, simply doing the right thing, is our most difficult problem and one of the chief secrets of abiding strength.

In the development of his judgment Lincoln unconsciously used the three great principles: humility, experiment, and that proposition in Euclid, that he learned early, the whole is greater than any one of its parts.

Humility comes first. We advance upon our knees. Lincoln was from the beginning to the end always anxious to learn, realizing his desperate need of learning. He was always modest, always disclaiming knowledge, always eager to acquire and use the knowledge of others. He succeeded in perhaps an unprecedented degree in getting himself out of the way that he might see clearly. He lived impersonally. Many of the men about him in his official life—Seward, Stanton, Chase, McClellan—thought little of him and took no pains to hide it, but that made no difference. He thought of them and their tasks. He thought. He did not feel or resent. He kept himself out of the way that he might think. He came to be—not he was immediately or by native endowment—he came to be one of the most successful judges of men that we have had in our national life because of just this quality of humility. He thought with his brain, not with his spleen. He looked out from himself, not through himself.

Humility is fundamental in learning how to think. And next is experiment. It might be called initiative, or trial and error, or, as we say usually, experience. Getting busy with the thing, trying it out, putting it into practice. We learn to crawl by crawling. It is the laboratory, the clinic, in modern education. So Lincoln did not shrink from life; he plunged in. He split rails, he ran boats, he kept store, he borrowed books, he swapped yarns, he fought, he entered military service, he studied law, he practiced law for twenty-six years. He learned to get along by getting along. He learned what men would do and what would happen under certain circumstances. He got into politics early—postmaster, county surveyor, legislature. He kept on running and kept on losing, but kept on learning. Then he began to win. He got into the National Congress. And before we can realize it he is running for the Senate and matching strength with the incomparable Douglas, before the State of Illinois—tens of thousands, driving out in wagons, camping, picnicking, looking, listening, straining with the wrestlers. We are surprised at Lincoln's emergence. But that is his way—forever putting the thing to the touch, building up always a mass of tested knowledge, like a scientist, to use in thinking.

So to humility we add experiment. Next, to the more difficult matter of distinguishing between the whole and its parts. "The whole is equal to the sum of its parts, and is therefore greater than any one of its parts." In the business of learning how to think nothing is more important. Lincoln got hold of that principle, and in one of the sternest tests that men have known it served him well.

Here is what I mean. In Washington, Lincoln sat the silent target of many attacks. The South was thundering one thing, the Northern Democrats another thing, Horace Greeley and the newspapers another, the abolitionists another, the politicians in his own party another, his official advisers another. Not that any group remained consistent. It was a time of divided councils. The one thing needed and awfully needed was the Thinker, who could hear all those cries quietly, soberly, evaluate each for what it was —a part—and in the midst of all of them, or out of all of them, or beyond all of them, find the whole. And, having found it, listen to it, interpret it, lead it. That was what Lincoln was able to do—to keep the whole before him and not let any part usurp that place. An exceedingly difficult thing, because the parts are right upon us and shouting at a terrible rate or whispering even more significantly, while the whole may have no coherent voice at all and may be hiding away in far places.

It was thus, it seems to me, that he held to slavery as an issue. He began with it and closed with it. Spliced between there was a period when his issue was the preservation of the Union. It was as far as he could go, he felt, and was the needed call for the time. But later, to whip the North to fighting edge and gain foreign support, he swings back to the old position. Good politics? Yes, because true thinking. In cold fact, the Union did not have to be preserved, but slavery had to go. That was the whole, the final, as against all the parts and all temporary expedients.

This discrimination between the whole and any of its parts may be said to base his realization that patience is the only way to work. Real growth is slow. Parts may spring up here and there and sprout for a day; the whole comes painfully but powerfully along. He sensed history as a continuity and learned how to detect the main stream.

Let me repeat that Lincoln had saving sense, judgment, and that he educated it by humility, experiment, and discernment of the whole as against its parts.

Now to gather up again, we have mentioned as secrets of Lincoln's power his oneness with the people and his capacity to think, his judgment. Two more must be added: his moral earnestness and his willingness to accept responsibility.

Moral earnestness. A man may know people fully and command unparalleled powers of discrimination and be a demagogue still, exalting only himself and misleading his fellows, and finally go out like a vanquished light leaving darkness and a stench. But from his young manhood Lincoln came into possession of a moral earnestness that marked him off from the ordinary ranks of men. It was no piosity, no parading of religious scruples or smug enforcement of religious motives, but a towering man feeling the final things.

In his debates with Stephen A. Douglas the contrast must have been strange indeed—the backwoods against the city, grotesqueness against urbanity—but there was another contrast deeper still. It was the final against the temporary, moral earnestness against expediency. Not that Douglas was immoral or an opportunist in public life, except by comparison with that Hebrew prophet who stood by him on those famous platforms. And the moral earnestness won. Douglas went to the Senate in 1858, but it was Lincoln who went to the Presidency in 1860. "I am not trying to entertain but to convince," was his reply to those who urged more of the popular note. "If you press that point," one said, "it will send Douglas to the Senate." "I know," Lincoln said, "but it will keep him out of the Presidency two years later." Right and Wrong came to be two great Lincoln words. They were the words upon which he ended the Cooper Union speech, which probably gave him the Presidency.

Lincoln believed that he was answerable to God. "Jehovah, before whom I stand," he might have said in perfect simplicity, as he did many times in other words. A man of prayer, a man of silences, a man of few and chiseled words, a man of moral earnestness. The worldlings may say what they will, but the men of God do the work.

Willingness to take responsibility. Early in Lincoln's presidential incumbency Seward wrote him a remarkable letter suggesting a number of policies and saying that somebody must lead the country, which was by way of a modest presentation of himself. Lincoln replied, not mentioning the suggested policies, some of which were foolish in the extreme, but acknowledging that leadership was indeed necessary and adding that he himself, having been chosen for the responsibility, must assume it. And he did. He did his own thinking. He listened to everybody and followed nobody. He was called a despot and a weakling by turns. "That clown in the White House." Nobody was pleased. "Without a friend in Washington," was said once. Probably no other President was ever so despised. But he bore his load; he went his way.

It is of the nature of responsibility that ultimately one man must bear it. Autocrats are falling off their old rotten thrones—autocrats in religion, in government, in industry. Government is of the people, but finally by a process of choosing one man stands out alone to bear the burden. It cannot be shirked. Leadership is not by committee. The wise man uses his committee, his board, his everything he can get in the way of councilors, but at last he himself, mantled with authority, must take his place in the Praetorium for the people to praise and execrate, to crown and crucify.

Events were kind to Lincoln. With his severe limitations, if his times had been ordinary, he might have lived and died an officeholder of second or third rank. And he might not. Who can say? At least it was a part of greatness to be ready when that one task for which he was fitted called. Again events were kind in his death. He died at the precisely right moment. That pistol shot and the fool jumping out of the theater box turned Lincoln's life into a drama. All the other elements were ready. It needed only that *dénouement.* It was not death that came to him, but a translation in a chariot of fire. Long since he has become a legend, a symbol, one of the gods in Humanity's temple. If he had lived, he might have gone out in tragic anticlimax. His fate in putting through his Reconstruction plans might have been the same as Andrew Johnson's. And yet again he might have added other glories to that strange Gothic structure. Was the cathedral really finished? At least it was greatness to have lived as long as he did in such fashion as that when Death came Immortality came along too to go on with the building.

ROBERT E. LEE.—The second year of the War my father ran away from school as a boy of sixteen and "joined the army," as he used to say, the army of Lee and Jackson. He was not a professional Southerner, had no rhetoric for the Lost Cause, took no part, that I can remember, in Confederate organizations, but he had unparalleled admiration and affection for Lee and Jackson. He used to stop our pulses and start them racing again with his stories of the two men, of the way the soldiers forgot their bleeding feet and empty stomachs when either of them rode down the lines. He loved to compare them, in appearance, in method of discipline, in manner of fighting, and in the places they occupied in the love of the army. After the Surrender—it was written with a capital and everything in adjacent years reckoned on it—he leaned his gun against a tree, hung his knapsack on it, and walked back home. But he never walked out from the sway of Lee and Jackson. Early and J. E. B. Stuart and A. P. Hill were brilliant and interesting, but they only adorned the picture of the other two. What a night it was when Jackson fell, and what a day when Lee came back from his conference with Grant. When we children sat in the firelight of winter evenings and listened, we used to wonder, at least I did, which he really loved the more, and when he talked about the one, I questioned if there were not treason in his heart against the other. But then he would set all right by quoting Lee in his letter to Jackson after Chancellorsville: "You have lost your left arm, but I have lost my right." "Jackson was Lee's right arm," he would say. "Ah, yes—Jackson to take a position, Lee to hold it; Lee to plan, Jackson to execute. Nobody knew Lee's mind like Jackson." Lee's mind, Lee's arm—Lee. I used to wonder about the crushing responsibility on one man to say that it was all over. "No, Lee said, go home, and we went." Whatever Lee said was right.

Curious how that boy spoke for the whole South. Whatever Lee said. That was the way they all felt. There were years when I discounted those firelight judgments as the beautiful imaginings of boyish hero worship, or as the natural yet nevertheless sectional interpretations of history. But I hark back to-day and find them sober statements of fact. The weight of unprejudiced and scientific opinion places Lee and Jackson among the greatest of the masters of war, and Lee, when the final shot was fired and in the years following, had an influence in the South almost beyond belief. And that influence was rooted in love.

How men loved him! And what a clear, unmixed love it was! It persisted and increased after all enthusiasm of the moment's victory and hope for the future were gone. And there was in it, of course, no vaguest trace of the expectation of any kind of gain. I have been sitting out among the trees by the side of my river—I have borrowed, you recall, several hundred feet of it—well, in these silences I have been reading some more about the great Southerner, particularly Gamaliel Bradford's measured study—measured but immeasurably moving. His chapter on Lee and the Army broke up the fountains of the deep for me. Just a plain narrative of how an army was treated by its leader and how it responded, both during the War and afterwards. A moving tale. Why? Because of the art in it? Yes, partly. Because of my associations? Yes, I suppose so undoubtedly. But mainly, it seems to me, it is moving because we all long to be loved and so few of us are. If that is superficial and some one prefers to say that we all long to possess those qualities which would make us loved—why, the two are the same. Love ought to be, it is so beautiful, so primary, so final, that when we actually see it, there is no adequate response but tears. It was so that Lee was loved by a whole army, a whole land.

Not all great men have great bodies by any means. But occasionally Nature in a happy mood shows us the ideal. Robert E. Lee had a great body. "He could assume no attitude that was not graceful." "Of Lee and Jackson, it was given to only one to look great." "I have seen all the great men of our times —and Robert E. Lee was incomparably the greatest looking of them all." "I had before me the most manly and entire gentleman I ever saw." "Men loved to gaze on him." "General Lee is the most perfect animal form I ever saw." "Remarkable beauty and attractive manners." "Not Pericles nor Washington would seem in this [that is, in body] to have been more royal than was Lee."

Now that body with its manner, its gestures, its attitude, its tone of voice, its expression of face, was the product of the best blood in America. Heredity in its many branches seemed in him to have conspired to produce a perfect man.

Shirley on the James is one of the finest of the early Virginia houses and the oldest. It was built about 1650 and its box and roses set out the same year. Jamestown was still the capital of Virginia when Shirley's famous staircase and paneling were brought over from England. They are famous now. The house is famous now and is a mansion yet, despite all our modern splendor. It is a symbol of all the glory that was, when Virginia was young. Its hospitable doors opened to the gallant and the beautiful. Its great halls resounded to the little and large things they talked about. Its chandeliers shone on their silks and brocades, their jewels and their swords.

At Shirley, one night, in the dining room, Anne Carter lifted a cut-glass bowl of strawberries. It was too heavy for her slender hands—supposedly—and she called for help. Light-Horse Harry Lee, distinguished even in that company, sprang to her assistance. That was the beginning of a courtship that ended in their marriage. He took her to Stratford, the family seat, and there Robert Edward was born on the 19th of January, 1807. Or so they tell it at Shirley. At any rate, the substantial facts are as stated. From such people and in the midst of such people Robert E. Lee was born. He is the ideal Virginian, the finest product of that aristocratic strain of our national culture, which came in through the mouth of the Chesapeake Bay and flourished along the Rappahannock, the Potomac, and the James Rivers in our Colonial and Revolutionary eras.

Some force came to Lee's aid, some genius in discrimination and direction, enabling him to escape the manifest perils of his body and his blood. How easily history might have dismissed him as simply another button on a beautiful coat, as a scion of great things gone, rather than a sire of great things to be.

Lee came to be, whether he was at first or not, entirely unaware of himself physically and uninterested in his pedigree. "The money had better be appropriated to help the poor," was his answer when some genealogist wanted to trace back his family lines.

Instead of the leisure, either elegant or gross, which he might have considered his native right, he applied himself definitely to a profession.

Instead of the pride of a great house, a great marriage, great estates, which would have been perfectly natural, we find in him as typical qualities modesty, gentleness, self-effacement, the forgiveness of injuries.

He let slip the accidents and deformities of his time and circumstance, and preserved the spirit of those spacious days. He was of the world of Washington. Love of liberty and courage were his, together with a certain stateliness, which cannot be described, but must be felt. Grace and charm were to him the essence of life. The manner of doing a thing was almost as important as the thing itself. Thus he has no word of criticism of his yesterdays. He merely walked through their palaces and bore away the treasures, leaving the rest.

The reason that men loved Lee was that he loved them. They followed him and were anxious to do his bidding because they felt that he suffered with them and for them. The more I read of Lee, the more I am impressed with the paternal element in him. He was a father to his men. He felt toward them as his children. And the wealth and beauty of his nature made them accept his fatherly care, as parched grass accepts the dew. I say wealth and beauty—I include in them sincerity. They knew that he meant more than he said. They knew that he was paying more dearly for the Cause than they could possibly pay, and that a part of his payment was his love for them. So that he came to represent the Cause to them, and they fought for him and died for him.

I do not think for a moment that Robert E. Lee was always what he was in late life. He was fifty-four years old when the Civil War and his fame began. And we look at him mainly through a glamour that came even after that.

His father was far from overprecise in his personal life, and Lee's own beautiful relationships with a number of charming women, in all probability, represent the ordered refinement of what might easily have been crude and ugly.

There are several early pictures all of them strikingly handsome, which show a light of mirth, and one perhaps a touch of haughtiness. The later pictures have no hint of these qualities, and the Lee of our common knowledge has already become the martyr of the Confederacy. We see him already on his pedestal, not climbing there.

We know him as the man of peace. His father,

however, was a man of war and loved war, and there are hints that Lee himself had that passion in him. A number of men have testified that there was a reckless strain in him that sometimes leaped into the saddle. Several have said that on one or two occasions they saw him with guard down, the calm gone, and battle in his eyes. He himself said once: "It is fortunate that war is so horrible, or we might come to love it."

His letters, moreover, tell us very little of himself. He does not unbosom. There are no secrets. There is never any gush of confidence. His past is not for the eyes of others. His inner is for himself alone. And there are no close friends. There were children. He never forgot his family and he was devoted to his comrades in the great strife. But he did not show himself in process of becoming himself to any of these. His heart layer on layer they never saw. It was only the top layer. Approachable Lee always was, but never approached. The meanest soldier could get to him, but the most intimate associate never found him unprotected. Only Traveller knew Lee, and Traveller wrote no memoirs.

The point I am trying to make is that Lee had to fight for what he achieved in character. He did not leap full-fledged into his stature of manhood. We get no record of his striving, save a hint here and there, but we feel that it went on, and we approach him therefore as human like ourselves and gather encouragement in our own toilsome trying to live the better life.

But we wonder about the battle and its issue in such fair achievement. Why did he begin it? What was its goal? How did he manage it? How did he bring it to its conclusion? What was the secret of his character, therefore of his power? How did he make men love him so that they wanted to die for him, despite his failure, and that men reading about him weep? How did he escape all the perils by the way and arrive at his destiny of undying influence?

Nobody knows the answer, of course. Perhaps he didn't know. And if he knew, he hasn't told us. Probably he never thought of himself as possessing power, only responsibility. That itself is a part of the secret, but how did he compass that achievement?

His mother and his wife were both invalids, so that nearly all his life he was schooled in tenderness. That undoubtedly had its influence, but he might easily have neglected them.

He chose a great cause that failed. That surely

culminated his training in character. But how did he make that decision, and how did he carry it through?

I believe that Robert E. Lee's secret was his conception of God. Easily the largest thing in his life was his religion, and I believe the controlling influence. He is the most religious man in our American life. The name of God appears more frequently in his letters and conversation than in those of any other man, that I know of, in public position. It is probable that that can be made to include those in private life as well, even ninety per cent of ministers. I have never read any other letters that spoke so often of prayer or of Christian privilege and duty.

Characteristically we know very little of the beginnings or of the processes of Lee's religious experience. We do know, however, as Gamaliel Bradford says, that it was not dependent upon ritual and not concerned with theology. It was of the most practical type. In connection with theology, however, I think it is true that Lee's faith dwelt in the Fatherhood of God. In his letters, that is predominant and endlessly recurrent—God's protecting care over his children. It was in this faith that Lee extended to the people of the South the arms of a father's love.

There may have been an earlier stage of thinking, in which he gained victory for personal life, but fatherhood is the final note in Lee's religious experience. Indeed, it may have been the first, for realization of place in God's family would have been effective then as later.

It was in this faith, I think, that Lee made his great decision and cast in his lot with Virginia and the Confederacy. Reason and self-interest called in the other direction. But he thought the liberties of his people transgressed, though he abhorred secession and had long since freed his own slaves. And "I could take no part in an invasion of the Southern States." That last decided the matter, and we know that, tragic as his situation was, there could have been no other choice.

It was this faith, I think, that bore him through the terrible years of the War in the manner and with the results already mentioned, and that sustained him in the final catastrophe.

It was this faith which transformed that catastrophe into his noblest achievement. He led and loved his people then as not before. Invited into many places of prominence, he chose the presidency of a small college to build the South back into the nation, beginning with its young manhood. And he gave himself there with no retarding of intelligence or devotion. He finished his course, and it wound upward till the last. In addition to his scholastic labors, an extensive correspondence carried his voice all over the South, with his conviction that now allegiance to the united nation was the only course for a man. He refused to defend himself, to discuss the past, or to harbor any bitterness. And so he led his people.

An English nobleman offered him a country seat in England and an annuity of $15,000. I know of nothing finer than his reply: "I must abide the fortunes and share the fate of my people."

Drinkwater catches this idea in his play on Lee. The closing words are from Peel, who has followed through the War.

"The dead, and a memory, and a hope. A name —Robert E. Lee. To-morrow we are going home. He is going with us."

THEODORE ROOSEVELT—WOODROW WILSON

In the period of the World War, Theodore Roosevelt and Woodrow Wilson inevitably emerge.

They were alike in many particulars. Their mothers were both Southern. They themselves sustained even an "in-law" relation. Mrs. George Howe, of Columbia, South Carolina, whose son married Woodrow Wilson's sister, was an aunt of Theodore Roosevelt's mother. (Don't stop to figure it out.) They both idolized their fathers. They both started with frail health. They both suffered from impaired vision, and both worse glasses from boyhood. They were both interested in athletics and, perforce in early days, in much the same way. They were both sketchy in college preparation, both impatient of curricular control, both only measurably distinguished in scholastic achievement, both great readers, both early and prolific writers. They were both Liberals in politics, and in both cases their earliest political mentors were Irish, though this may call for no particular mention in the United States. They were both enormous workers and by ordering their time produced enormous results. They were both blessed with great women for wives. They both enjoyed unbroken domestic happiness and were stainless in personal life. They were both religious, both Presbyterians. Neither died early enough to become immediately immortal. The foundations of both houses were crumbling, and the windows darkened long before the final crash came. True in both cases, especially perhaps in Wilson's.

Alike, yet how different. Wilson's education came out of colleges; Roosevelt passed through Harvard incidentally. Wilson stood in books and looked out, finally walked out. Roosevelt was out all the time, but carried his books with him bound in pigskin to protect them from the weather. Wilson entered politics late, fifty-four; Roosevelt never entered anything else. One was thus a statesman, the other a statesman and a politician. Roosevelt learned teamwork by early failures without it; Wilson, try as he might, could never get down from his isolated peak. One was emotional, the other intellectual—evangelist and theological professor. One was versatile, the other one-tracked. One was dramatic, the other didactic. One loved nature; the other was apparently unaware. Both beginning frail, one entered the White House with "a quart of headache tablets and a stomach pump," the other with the body of a giant and an equipment of boxing gloves and wrestling mats. Wilson fished for his friends in a trout brook with a fly, then let nearly every one go. Roosevelt used a dragnet and kept all. Roosevelt had one man in his skin, Wilson two. Roosevelt plowed straight on from the beginning; Wilson began to walk the floor at Princeton and say, "I must go out and do something." The capitol city of Theodore Roosevelt's life was action. The capitol city of Woodrow Wilson's life was thought. His action was in order to quiet matters and then go back and think some more.

Never did the lives of two men more definitely enforce the truth that power does not come through being like somebody else. Here were the two, in the same position, doing essentially the same thing, and yet developing their prodigious power by such diverse methods that Roosevelt spent his last strength in a vituperation of Wilson, which we may well forget, and Wilson, though more fortunate in self-control, certainly never regarded Roosevelt as one of his favorites.

THEODORE ROOSEVELT.—In his time Theodore

Roosevelt was the best-loved man in the United States and possibly the best-loved man that ever was in the United States. "The most popular president since Washington," Thayer says. Well, that is conservative. Everything was a Teddy in those days from women's garments to children's playthings. Bears still name their children after him. People in far waste places stayed up late and rose early merely to wave at his train as it passed. He was the typical American, and men loved him as they loved themselves made splendid in their dreams. And in proportion to his popularity was his power. He was the dominant figure of his country and of the world.

How did he do it? What was his secret? Prying into his life, what do we find?

In the first place, he was the most *Picturesque* figure that has ever appeared in our national life.

Reading his life, it is at times impossible to escape the illusion that we are following, not a flesh and blood man, but a boy's hero fashioned by some master of the imagination. He comes and goes perfectly at home among the shades of Diamond Dick, Nick Carter, Old King Brady, Old Sleuth. Then for a moment Richard the Lion-Heart and Charlemagne are with us and Roland and Oliver. I have been reading him again out in the woods, and two or three times I have found myself saying: "It is all perfectly simple. This is the American epic. Other races and ages have with the inspired consent of unseen singers bodied themselves forth in the exploits of single men. This is America I am reading about now—life in its latest adventure, in its newest invasion of the darkness."

Every boy in my little town planned seriously at intervals to run away and go west. Fighting Indians, riding all day and sleeping on your saddle, chasing buffalo, facing grizzlies, wearing buckskin and two guns, delivering crisp ultimatums to gamblers and killers, bringing evildoers to justice—that was the picture. A whole literature sprang up out of that life, and at least half an art, and more recently both together in the movies. We read about it and dreamed about it then; we look at it now. Roosevelt did it—all of it. Not one chapter did he leave out. He was in at the making.

But your true man is at home everywhere, and your Western hero doesn't hesitate to skip east every now and then to straighten out a State or clean up a city. Everything he did was in the key of those Western adventures—leading the Rough Riders to

Cuba, sending the fleet around the world, attacking the "malefactors of great wealth." His whole method was dramatic; his vocabulary itself was like his fringed buckskins. Being President was the same sort of experience as being a cowboy. And he is no sooner out of the White House than he is off to Africa hunting and exploring, and no sooner through with the Bull Moose campaign than he is down in the wilds of South America enduring privations that were too much even for his stalwart health.

Striving for picturesqueness is play-acting and desperately silly business. But Roosevelt was simply living his life out. The secret of his picturesqueness was daring to be himself. On the other hand, there are certain academic souls who consider it virtue to be drab and refuse to throw their personalities into anything. The demagogue exploiting himself has frightened many of us into not using ourselves.

Observe next his *Courage*.

His father conducted his family in such a manner as to preserve that fine balance between confidence and respect for others. It was a little democracy in which every citizen had inalienable rights. That was the beginning of Roosevelt's courage. He was not quashed in childhood. But even so, he had to study and learn courage. In boyhood he was afraid by reason of his frail constitution and weak vision. Later he was afraid. He tells us that there were many things in the West that he was afraid of—grizzlies, mean horses, two-gun men—but by acting as if he were not afraid he lost his fear. The sight of him, kneeling and shooting as he is charged by a bear powerful enough and fierce enough to kill a horse with one stroke of his paw, is surely tonic for weak hearts. But that came with practice. In the same way in political life he quietly received the rush of many a foe more formidable than a grizzly bear. "Only those are fit to live who do not fear to die, and none are fit to die who have shrunk from the joy of life and the duty of life." The thrill in those words is that they were minted out of the metal of his own living.

His trip out of Africa and through Europe provides many examples of his courage. When he reached Egypt, Boutros Pasha, the Prime Minister, had just been openly assassinated by a member of the Nationalist party. Roosevelt was asked to speak at the University of Cairo, but warned to say nothing of Boutros Pasha, as feeling was divided and dangerously high. He replied: "You are at perfect liberty to withdraw your invitation, but if I speak I shall certainly mention him." He did and in no uncertain terms. The result was electrical. He was cheered to the echo.

As he approached Rome he was invited to an audience with the pope with the quiet stipulation that he was not to visit the Methodist Mission in the city. He replied that he could not accept an invitation which in any way limited his freedom of conduct. He did not see the pope.

In Paris he propounded one of his favorite doctrines of adequate families, though, or more properly because, he was in a country of declining birth rate.

In London he delivered his Guildhall speech urging Britain either to govern Egypt or to get out. "Govern or go."

Yet Roosevelt was far from impulsive. He was no candidate for cracking his head against a wall. He thought out his course carefully, sought advice from every source, and, having decided, went hard, forgetting himself. But back of that decision was definite planning. Lawrence Abbott knew him possibly as well as any other man and lists caution as one of his outstanding characteristics.

But courage he had in eminent degree—magnificent, red, and raw. The courage of being himself unqualifiedly and of flinging himself in without any reserve whatsoever.

"The Lion is dead," was the death message which the two boys in France received from their brother at home.

Under the head of Roosevelt's *Humanity* many things must be grouped. His religion falls here. It was a faith of the square deal to every man. The inner was carefully guarded, the outer was for all eyes. James E. Amos, his negro personal servant through many years, *supposes* that he was a member of the Dutch Reformed Church, but he adds, "He was the most thoroughly Christian man I have ever met." A regular attendant at church, a reader of the Bible, a lover of the old hymns, his humanity appears in his regard for the faiths of all men and for men of all faiths.

His obedience falls here—his love of law and his determination to enforce it and follow it. His servants speak of what they choose to call his obedience, meaning his gentleness at home and his desire to observe the rules of the family life.

His humanity was the basis of his teamwork—he was able to work with all kinds and degrees of men—

and of the remarkable wealth of his friendships—statesmen, authors, artists, cowboys, farmers, policemen, pugilists, princes. Roosevelt was consistently a party man, a team man all his life. His staying by his party when Blaine was nominated was of a piece with his bolting his party in 1912. When he led the Progressives he felt that the Republican party, properly speaking, was with him and not with Taft, both in numbers and in principles. And the popular vote showed that he was right, certainly in the first instance.

His humanity was the basis of his public policy, both national and international. Labor and capital represented human beings to him. He was perhaps the first of our great public men to talk about Industrial Democracy—giving labor a share in the profits and the management of business. The Chinese Indemnity and the Cuban situation were handled on the simple human plane. He preached that the dealings of nations ought to regard identically the same morals as the dealings of individuals. His greatest achievement was probably in cleansing and exalting all branches of the government service, and that grew out of his simple faith that since we are all men here together it is silly and criminal to let a few prey on the rest.

Humanity was his passion and in considerable measure his explanation. He was not above it but of it, not beyond it but within it. Nothing human was strange to him, and nothing human but moved him one way or another. It is inaccurate to say that he loved humanity; he was simply a part of humanity, everywhere and all sorts. He loved the outgoings of its hope, the leaping and swelling of its courage, the dust and sweat of its battles.

His attitude toward peace was a part of his human passion. He was a genuine lover of peace and was quite ready to fight for it. In fact, his emphasis was on that last, which was almost inevitable, given his disposition and his experience. On the American stage, which means the world stage, and in the period before us, Wilson had the final word with reference to peace just as he had with reference to progressive legislation, and I think that history will accord him the victory in the debate. After all, peace by peaceable methods is better than peace through war. Roosevelt enjoyed war as he enjoyed all life. Wilson did not.

The last quality in Roosevelt, which I shall mention, is *Action.* Without that all things else are upholstery and body without motor. A charge of powder will drive a candle through a two-inch board. The missile is not so important; it is the stuff behind it. There are only two classes of men—those who do something about it and those who do not. We all know enough and feel enough to begin with. Action is the determining factor. Jesus pressed that home over and over again. Roosevelt was the executive personified. He was decision on two legs. "Niagara and President Roosevelt impressed me in America," said John Morley.

He did something about his body. He had none and built one. And having built it, he drove it as scarcely any other man ever drove a body.

His writing was in this realm. He wrote about men and the doing of things—"Life of Benton," "Life of Gouverneur Morris," "Life of Cromwell," "The Naval War of 1812," "The Winning of the West." And more of it was about his own doings—in the West, in Africa, in South America. And interminable letters.

And the manner of his writing was in this realm. Never a busier man, yet always writing. Not, "I would like to write"—"I am writing." In the West, horseback all day, going the absolute limit with men who fell into their bunks at night—yet writing. In Africa, boring through the jungle, in South America —writing. Campaigning for Governor of New York —writing a book. As Governor—writing a book. As President—writing a book.

He said to the students at Oxford that he was an ordinary horseman, an ordinary hunter, an ordinary intellect, an ordinary man. And so he was, but driven by an extraordinary will. The candle with the charge of powder behind it. The measure of a man is not his capacities, but the use he makes of them. And as God sees, the measure of a man is not the bulk or apparent importance of his achievements. It is a question of the development of the power that in him lies. Roosevelt there ranks near the top, and the four qualities which I have ventured to name as explaining him are Picturesqueness, Courage, Humanity, Action.

WOODROW WILSON.—It is probable that our eyes have actually seen in Woodrow Wilson a great man, an immortal man. Probable that the League of Nations will catch his name up among history's darlings. Probable that he and Washington and Lincoln will go down to the future as the three Titans thus far thrown up out of the life stuff of this American people.

Your true fighting man. For democracy in education at Princeton, for democracy in the State of New Jersey, for democracy in the United States of America, for democracy among the nations of the world. Always jousting against privilege and for the oppressed. And always seeing to it by the height of his aims that he lost. And yet always winning, for he fought on the side of Destiny.

His record is written in legislation and institution at Princeton, at Trenton, at Washington, and at Geneva; in educational and state papers which were spiritual pronouncements for his time. He fought with carnal weapons, but not mainly. Probably never such movement of men and material as when the die was finally cast. But the real struggle and the real areas of battle were not for men's eyes. A thousand agencies brought from the ends of the earth the distillations of men's hearts that he might further distill and reveal the world to itself. Always the schoolmaster, the wielder of words, the debater. "I'll argue this out with you in the Senate." But it was before the world that he finally argued out the great matters. Allies in the trenches, the British Navy on the sea, and Woodrow Wilson in the air. One-third of credit to each. William Allen White says: the armies in the field, England's navy enforcing famine on the homeland, and Wilson talking to the German people. Other conquerors have sent before them the wolf of hunger or the dragon of fear. Wilson released the dove of peace.

He undoubtedly clarified the vision and quickened the life of the vast, hidden masses of the earth.

He overcame and was for a day the ruler of the world to an extent and in a manner that no other man ever was. And it may be that he waits but a little before coming back to his throne.

In the man walks the boy.

"Tommy" Wilson was always frail, therefore always "Tommy," never "Tom." As a child he crushed a finger, which left it stiff for life—another link in the chain which bound him to the shallows or to the deck of only dream galleons. But worst of all, he wore glasses.

In his boyish imagination he brought down redskins with his trusty bow, organized a baseball team, and sailed a pirate ship, the Avenger. The significant things in the connection, however, are that he kept the log of the Avenger for three months and that the baseball team was also a sort of debating club which developed a high parliamentary technique.

No fights are chronicled against Tommy Wilson, or he might have been Tom. Boyhood friends tell of his throwing down his bat and leaving the field rather than submit to injustice, but never of his resorting to the arbitrament of hair-pulling, pommelling, kicking, scratching—and the epic tale of it later—or the labored explanation.

But many things go to make up that boy who afterwards walks in the man. Not only spectacles and smashed fingers and frail health. Things like fine old columned houses; life among the aristocratic best of earlier small Southern cities, Augusta, Georgia, Columbia, South Carolina; dignified, handsome, brilliant parents; Scott, Dickens, Lamb read aloud at home; family prayers; the Church the center of everything; indulgence as given to the youngest, especially a boy.

The American Presbyterian Church that Tommy Wilson knew was under Southern leadership. Thornwell and Palmer were the giants, and they were familiars in his father's house. They, with Moses

D. Hoge, met in his father's study to confer about the division which the Civil War was making inevitable. The formal organization took place in his father's church. Young as he was, Tommy Wilson saw these men and movements and thrilled, though vaguely, to be, in a sense, a part of the inner circle when history was moving.

The Civil War did not reach him. The only members of his family actively engaged were far to the north and on the other side. His father was a chaplain, his uncle in the chemistry division. War heroes, however, walked past, and he never forgot—Alexander H. Stephens and Jefferson Davis on their way to prison, and later Robert E. Lee, who became one of his permanent heroes.

When he was fourteen his father went to Columbia, South Carolina, as professor in the Theological Seminary. There the war burst full on the boy—never as glory, always as tragedy. Columbia's business section, three blocks wide and a mile long, lay a blackened ruin, and the legislature was full of field negroes herded on by scalawags. The twin horrors, war and a vindictive peace, were burnt into his thinking from that day.

In the man walks the boy. But the boy is not

alone. He is surrounded by a great company of those who have lived before and built the blood, dead long since, most of them, yet living, laughing, hating, loving, struggling, fighting, singing, suffering in the man, who for the time being bears all of them toward the future and some sort of divine far-off event.

Woodrow Wilson will never be understood until one looks through the Wilson of him back into the stream of his father's people and through the Woodrow of him back into the stream of his mother's people. One of those streams is Irish—imaginative, dreaming, varicolored, quick-tempered, generous brilliant, talkative, musical, full of pun and quip and strut and prance. His father was like that—big, eloquent, handsome, courtly, demonstrative, affectionate, vain in spots. "My precious son"—he begins to his boy, who even then was a college professor. Moderator of the Assembly of his Church, Stated Clerk for thirty-eight years. "A ripe and racy Irish gentleman," one writes who knew him. "Ariel beginning to grow gray." "An aristocrat by the divine right of his cloth and the royal grant of his Irish blood."

A lovely old chap, if one ever drew breath. Up at Princeton once, when he thought he was dying, he sent for the three girls, his granddaughters, and said: "I want you girls to remember that your father is a very great man."

After one of his Princeton visits he was talking to Dave Bryant, an old negro family servant.

"Dave, are you still voting?"

"Yas, sir."

"Well, I want to make a request of you. Mr. Tommy is a very smart man. He is one of the smartest men in the world. Some day he is going to be President of the United States. If I am not alive when he runs, I want you to cast my vote for him—my vote, not yours."

It may have been this same Dave Bryant, who, when Woodrow Wilson finally came into the Presidency, said: "Well, Mr. Tommy he got de office, but de old Doctor he had de ways."

A host of witnesses testify that the "Old Doctor" handed along into the keeping of his boy his and his forbears' wealth of Irish charm. Woodrow Wilson was interested in athletics, devised football plays, led college yells; sang, went about in various places, Princeton, Virginia, Johns Hopkins, organizing glee clubs; loved good talk and stories and limericks and play. He was Irish in his college years—loved the life of a student and made men love him. Irish in his years of teaching—Bryn Mawr, Wesleyan, Princeton—voted over and over the most popular man on the Princeton faculty. Irish in his New Jersey experience—when he stepped on the stage of the Taylor Opera House before that new animal to him, a political convention, and accepted its nomination to the governorship. The Irish kings were there in their newest prince. The "Old Doctor" was there come into a better than his own. "Tones so soft, so fine; . . . voice so heart-stirring; . . . rhythm of his vigorous sentences; . . . swirling mass of men. . . . 'Thank God, at last a leader has come!' " Irish in the whole gay, electric, smashing campaign and in the short incumbency that followed, when promises were kept in true knightly fashion; day-dreams written into laws, selfish interests unhorsed, men's hearts stirred. A fantastic Irish joke, all of it, turning their own hose on the bosses just exactly as he said he would when they offered it to him. "You're no gentleman!" "You're no judge." "Woodrow Wilson, the next President of the United States."

Irish he was in much of that first term—the zest of great achievement, family and friends about him.

Dave Bryant—scarcely able to believe the fairy story —"I want you girls to remember that your father is a very great man." He always was Irish to the little group close about him. He bloomed under their love and appreciation and gave himself like a boy to their affection.

But not only Irish. There is another strain in him. Woodrow. Scotch. Scotch Presbyterian preachers with a few intermissions for five hundred years. Strong, pious, and scholarly all the way. All the Woodrows are alike in certain qualities; but we must look at one—not his mother, for life then held a woman somewhat in abeyance. His uncle rather—James Woodrow.

James Woodrow—Jefferson College, Harvard, Heidelberg; preacher, college professor, chief of medical laboratory, Confederate government, editor of two Presbyterian papers, Secretary Foreign Mission Board. Tried for teaching evolution; exonerated by Church, but lost theological professorship. President of bank. President of State University. Much of this carried at same time. Meanwhile member of scientific societies in America, Switzerland, England, Germany. A man of parts.

But more. This from one who knew him: "He

delegated nothing—read his own proof, unlocked his own office, taught his own classes, kept his own missionary books, fought a lone fight, never compromised. Lived here fifty years, but not a close friend in town. Too busy. Detached. No recluse—did a full man's part, but not with the crowd. Most punctual man I ever saw—never a minute early or late. Lived by rule. Dauntless fighter, but scorned to win crookedly."

There is your Woodrow blood—efficient, looking for the facts, impeccable, punctual, uncompromising, self-sufficient, isolated, emotional but silent, Scotch, dour.

In Woodrow Wilson's life the Irish and Scotch strains, the Wilson blood and the Woodrow blood grappled. The Wilson in him fought hard, but the Woodrows were strong, stern, and stubborn, and as the days closed about him with their travail and tragedy the inevitable happened. It was a Woodrow who fought at Princeton and in the War years a Woodrow sat in the White House, managed the world, and showed often to his own people a hard face.

In the man walks the boy. In the man walks the past of his blood. And in the man walks his God.

Woodrow Wilson, when the last is said about him,

was the product of his religion. His family on both sides ran back through long lines of preachers. His life was cradled in the things of God. And the God of his fathers became to him and continued till the last the vital and controlling experience of his life. Many men have spoken of his public prayers. He prayed privately every day upon his knees. He said grace at meals. He wore out two or three Bibles. He wrote much and talked much about the vital and personal things of religion.

Calvinism finally wrought itself out in his thinking and living in two great articles: First, God is sovereign and cannot fail; I will follow him without fear. Second, the cause of the people is the cause of God; I will serve it with all that I have.

Any interpretation of the power of this man which leaves out God uncouples the engine from the string of cars. His faith drove him. And he never lost it —faith in God, faith in people. He saw God so clearly that he sometimes overlooked men standing by him; he had his eyes so fixed on the people that individuals often escaped him; he was so dedicated as an instrument of God and the people that he forgot that others might be instruments too.

He never lost his faith. As "the lame lion of S

Street," when it seemed that America and Europe, all groups, cliques, cabals, all circumstances, the very stars in their courses had conspired to crush him, he still held on.

"You can't fight God."

"We are winning, Cecil, we are winning; hold fast, don't compromise."

"We're right, Baker, we're right; that's enough; don't fear the outcome; we're right."

PAUL, THE APOSTLE

PAUL had many and manifest weaknesses.

His body was evidently a poor thing. A mean personal presence he acknowledges to one of the groups, to whom he wrote, taking the words out of their mouths. Accordingly he was much stronger in writing than in speaking. Apollos was the orator of the apostolic era, not Paul.

In addition to being unimpressive, Paul's body was racked with some kind of disease, which was first acute, then chronic—or there may have been two distinct troubles. There are a number of references to attacks which prevented his carrying plans into execution. One of these was probably the occasion of his coming into first contact with Luke, the physician. Luke continued with him almost constantly after that, probably not only as a disciple but as medical attendant, indicating that Paul's sickness was a constant burden and threat. Then there is the reference to the "thorn in the flesh," from which he prayed deliverance three times and finally accepted as inevitable.

Blindness would seem to have been the difficulty,

the "thorn in the flesh." There might easily have been certain violent seizures in the beginning issuing in a permanently dimmed world. The main argument for blindness is Paul's not writing his letters, but signing them, to prevent imposture and to add a personal note, as we do to-day. "The salutation of Paul with mine own hand, which is the token in every epistle," he says to the Thessalonians. To the Galatians he writes: "Ye see with what large characters I have written unto you with mine own hand." And surely it is significant that he says to those same Galatians: "Ye would have plucked out your own eyes and given them to me, if it had been possible." Not necessary, possible. George Matheson, himself blind, has developed the thesis of Paul's blindness with great sensitiveness and minuteness.

A poor body and a weak body. And a limited mind.

Paul never got away from pharisaism in argument. He never became a universal in intellectual approach. The contention that woman is less than man, because she was created later and because through her came sin, is without point to-day. His great common sense broke from that when he wrote that the wife was not her own but the husband's, and the husband not his own but the wife's. He never got away from the magical in world culmination. The trump was to sound and bodies to be raised. Yet again, his argument in the fifteenth chapter of First Corinthians is far distant from that idea and purely spiritual. He never got away from the expectation of Christ's return in his generation. His usual advice about marriage is rooted here. Yet once more his heart has conquest over his mind, and he takes the Thessalonians to task for stopping work to await Christ's appearance.

The modern criticism, however, that Paul complicated the simple matter of Christianity is, I think, unjust. He was interpreting Christianity to his age and used the language that they knew. He simply leaped into the stream and fought the current and the eddies as they came.

Nor is Paul responsible for medievalism in the specific doctrine of the atonement. He did not confine the cross to the analogy of the court room. The medievalists did that. He used everything—placating monarchs, buying prisoners out of slavery, the school, the family. But more especially the whole impact of Paul is a thousand miles distant from legalism. With him form is nothing, life is everything.

Nobody with a free mind, reading Paul, ever got the notion of method or machinery or plan or technicality. Salvation is a divine and vital impartation, heavenly fire loosed in human life. "The life of God in the soul," is a summation of Paul's conception of religion.

Further, there must be listed among Paul's limitations his disposition to fanaticism, together with its record of murderous persecution against the new sect. That record kept him for a while out of the inner council of the Christians, stared him in the face always, and, with an ordinary man, would have been a serious impediment. The fanatical disposition, coming under the sway of Christ, was turned from destruction to beneficence, changed from fire to light. Yet, even so, it was a narrow escape for Paul that he did not use the same methods to bring men in that he had used to keep them out. With the slightest twist in his thinking about the essentials of Christian doctrine, Paul would have been an inquisitor, seeking to compel with prison and sword.

Despite his limitations, however, there is no greater example of power than Paul presents, with the single exception of his Master.

He was the organizing, shaping, and forwarding influence of the infant Church. Historically he was the founder of Christianity. He nursed the flame and set it going in the ancient cities. He led the little ragged army that went out to conquer the earth. He was greater in conquest than Alexander or Cæsar or both, for he overcame both.

What were the hiding places of his power?

Coming fresh to Paul, either casually or inquiring as to the sources of his influence, I think one would be struck, first, by his poetic passion. There is a Paul, the organizer; there is a Paul, the thinker. But both are caught up and fused and flashed about by Paul, the poet. He is never long on the ground. He begins a statement or an argument calmly enough, but presently his wings are beating the air. The effort to reduce such breathings of flame to theological syllogisms is full of ironic futility. Never anything more amusing, had it not been attended with such loss to the world and such crippling of a great spirit. As soon try to weigh a nightingale's song or reduce to parallelograms the flight of a condor across the Andes. Argument is worthless unless it burns. Facts are dead that are not tipped with fire.

As Paul grew older he grew more and more the poet. The "afternoon epistles" are quieter, but they move in a far more ethereal region. There are fewer leapings from the ground because there are fewer descents to the ground. One of the methods by which he managed to keep the gates open was silence. Paul did not usually seek silence, but God in great goodness gave it to him. There were the three years in Arabia at the beginning of his ministry; there were the two years in prison at Cæsarea; there were the terms of imprisonment at Rome; there were the various sicknesses. Whenever he speaks after one of these experiences there is the evidence of growth toward a surer intuition. Other men reason or feel or quote. The poet sees. And the gates are open in silence.

A second contribution to Paul's power was his imagination. Imagination is a very practical quality. It is possessed by all successful engineers, architects, business men. It is the capacity to see a thing in vision before it becomes a fact. It is the blue print of the building. It is the bridge swung in airy substance over the river, before the labor of construction has begun. It is the real estate development, with streets and houses and automobiles and people, swimming in the mind while the physical eye sees only a woodland. The ordinary man of Paul's time saw a world about him of men and things. It was the only world he had ever seen or expected to see. Paul brings to that world his imagination—or as he would have called it, his faith—and he sees it changed until under the domination of Christ. He sees peoples bending before the King invisible; he sees kings owning allegiance to the King of kings. Instead of hate he sees love; instead of war he sees peace; instead of sin he sees righteousness. Instead of defeat and despair he sees victory in the Son of God.

Now, Paul's imagination was not any mere vaporing of the mind. It presented a vision to be realized. He was a practical builder—to see was to begin doing. And he threw himself into the making of that new earth which his imagination had drawn for him. "I must also see Rome."

Here is the explanation of his confidence. The world of the first century had its religions already intrenched, its ways of thinking set for centuries. It was an august and imposing world. Now comes the new conqueror, hammering at the gates, claiming mastery, and with no weapon but a story. Little Paul. Rare confidence. But perfectly natural for Paul, because the new kingdom, set up by his imagination, was so clear and substantial that he could not doubt.

A third source of Paul's power was the scars he could show. He was not calling others to sacrifices which he had not made. His challenge was to an enterprise bathed in his own blood. The scars of the veteran are eloquent beyond all language. Paul had them. He bore in his body the marks of the Lord Jesus. His shipwrecks and imprisonments and scourgings and stoning said more convincingly than the tongues of angels that his message had first plowed through his own soul. And men could but listen.

The chief secret of Paul's power, however, was that he believed that Christ lived again in him. His conversion on the way to Damascus was the beginning of that experience and was in the nature of a revelation of the living Christ. The outward circumstances do not change the fact. He described the occurrence more and more simply as he grew older, till finally he said: "It pleased God to reveal his Son in me." If it came with an epileptic seizure, I am not concerned. The method of vision is not the test; it is the result in life. And Paul's life was changed root and branch by what happened on the Damascus road.

Nor do I find Paul's idea of the indwelling Christ mystically forbidding. History has proceeded in that way. Alexander is explained by his seeking to live again the life of Achilles. Julius Cæsar probably awoke from his life of a scented fop about Rome to the iron career of a conqueror through reading the exploits of Alexander, and his latest dream of a Parthian invasion was in imitation of his hero. Charlemagne in turn followed Cæsar, though a new influence is making itself felt in him. Napoleon is an absurd anachronism because he was trying to ircarnate conquerors too long dead.

Our weakness has come from inviting lesser persons to live in us. Paul's power came from the fact that he chose more wisely.

JESUS OF NAZARETH

JESUS has become the touchstone of human character. Unconsciously, but inevitably, every man coming into the world is dragged before him and stands or falls according to the silent judgment of his perfections. He is the judge of all the earth, inasmuch as he has erected a standard for human life, and that standard abides to damn or bless. The world is not his by any means; but in the final emergencies of our living, when we face all the stark, primal facts, we know that he is right and seek to square our characters with his.

I recall, as a boy, reading the "Count of Monte Cristo" and realizing vaguely that it struck a false note. Vengefulness is not the highest art, since Jesus has lived and set the opposite pattern. He imported into our estimate of the heroic new elements of gentleness and magnanimity. He peers over the shoulder of every bookmaker and playwright, and they know that, whatever other canons they may disregard, if their work is to live it must be done in the spirit of Jesus.

It has come to this, that there are only two plots. One is the realization of the self, the other the giving of the self away. And the first is usually but a stepping-stone to the second. Your literary craftsman works and reworks that theme in infinite variety. He builds a high stage for his action, he constructs majestic movement, he wraps it all about with an atmosphere of inevitableness, and then the hero does the one thing he can do since Jesus has lived—forgets himself. And the world, pit and gallery, laughs and shouts and sings and cries and thrills to its deepest depths with the ancient, universal, only theme—self-renunciation.

Even the love motive is no other than this. A man and a woman are built each to royal stature of strength and grace. Each stands a pattern of nobility, each adequate to all possible demands. Then come the beauty and tenderness of yielding. Each hears the call of the other nature and answers in rendering up the self. Never mind that they enter the new world under wreathed gates and garlanded arches and to the pleasings of lute and viol. That world is the world of self-renunciation, and they know it. Self-finding, then self-giving, and self thereby more fully found. Imperial persons bending in imperial forgetfulness of self—that is the requirement which Jesus has laid upon art and life.

Jesus of Nazareth is time's great example of such qualities as sincerity, magnanimity, loyalty, chivalry. By these he drew men in his short life, as the moon draws the tide, and has ever since, and will.

Circumstances besought him to accommodate his message. Threats of failure and coming peril added their voice. But sincerity forbade. He saw and must speak as he saw. He could not trim. "Hard sayings," they told him, but he would not trifle with his vision, or save himself, or win temporary success by any shadow of turning. "Will ye also go away?" he asked sadly, but he did not say that he would change even so much as emphasis to keep them.

His forgiveness of injury and his prayer for forgiveness sprang simply and naturally out of a nature too magnanimous to cherish bitterness. The petty, the spiteful, the vengeful, the remembrance of evil found no rootage in his mind. God's cleansing air blew all the way through all the time.

Loyalty is greater than courage because it includes courage and exalts it into unselfishness. Courage may end in the self; loyalty is for others. Loyalty subdues the individual champion to the harness of the group. Courage may be a performance merely; loyalty is a crusade. Greatest of qualities, it has been said. Jesus possessed it in rare degree and of rare kind. He gathered about him a little company and remained loyal to them. We speak vaguely and largely of Jesus loving the world. We should have known nothing of this had that love not manifested itself in his loyalty to those few who were about him. Love may have world implications but after all is personal.

There is a tradition that Jesus was invited to leave Palestine and accept the hospitality of Greece. And certainly the visit of the Greeks, in his last week, as told by John, looks in that direction. Whatever they may have said, his response was: "Except a corn of wheat . . . die, it abideth alone: but if it die, it bringeth forth much fruit." Such an answer would fit perfectly any suggestion on their part that he leave Palestine and Jerusalem and his little band and go and live with people who would appreciate him. Why not? His loyalty said, No. Loyalty to his countrymen, to his message, to his Father—but I think all of those he saw in the faces of that clinging few.

But perhaps the most beautiful thing in Jesus, and the most beautiful thing our eyes have ever beheld, was the chivalrous way he treated those who could not defend themselves—children, publicans, forsaken women. More beautiful than Oriental tapestry, or Grecian urn, or lacy stone or cathedral spire, or lily leaning with the breeze in a garden, or sea, or mountain, or sky, the fairest treasure we have in the records of the race is the treatment that Jesus accorded the little ones of the world. He turned away from kings and chose the weak for comrades. He called the unfortunate to walk with him in the way. He lifted up the losers and promised them other races and laurel wreaths. His age said, "Spurn." He said, "They are my younger brothers and sisters."

His confidence in humanity was a part of his chivalry. He went about saying to men and women: "Your heart and the world have betrayed you into a wrong estimate of yourself. It is a case of mistaken identity. The real you is not what now appears. The real you, that is to be, is of the family of God, strong and true and good." He did not go his way, with yardsticks and dry rules, convicting men; he carried keys to open their prison doors. He classified not according to present failures, but according to memories and dreams. He took for granted the royal intents of persons, and they were surprised into nobility by his expectations. Yet he was no romanticist. He simply refused to deal with people except on the basis of their true selves. He was a realist. He dealt with the real. If in abdication of the throne one addressed him, his response was nevertheless to the throne. He never gave back what one sent unless one sent the best. Thus men and women were spiritually born under his influence. He called them into blossom, like the sun speaking to flowers, each one coming into separate and sovereign beauty—lily and hollyhock and rose and violet. Jesus was the Prince of the realm of those who call out the best in others.

The infinite worth of personality—that was the basis of his feeling toward men. Burn palaces, dash priceless vases to the ground, topple kingdoms over, but do not bruise or hurt or warp in any smallest way the soul of a little child. There was no compromise here: nothing on earth was of any value at all except in relation to persons. A beguiling thing just to watch him walking so delicately among men lest he mar any least of them.

However, it is not chiefly in individual elements of character that Jesus is preëminent, but in the balance. Greatness hangs in the counter-position of the parts, in the fine poise which lets not any go too far before, nor any lag too far behind; not in particular brilliances, but in the teamwork of the soul. Observe, for example, how Jesus was able to live with and for the sinner without condoning his sin; or how, infinitely removed from flattery, he was yet able to express confidence in men. He thought and spoke and acted as one Spirit moving outward toward expression. "Forgive your enemies," was his teaching; and without any self-consciousness he forgave his when need arose. His putting his finger on love as the secret of life, after the centuries of philosophic groping, is like nothing so much as the sun coming up over the hills. But his life, illustrating that principle, is like light taking a body and coming to dwell among us. His life bore testimony to an unshaken inner harmony. Mind, emotion, will were one. He desired according to his judgment and willed according to his desire. He went through seasons of fearful stress, but the struggle attested only the fury of the storm, and the safe issue in each instance proved the integrity of the soul that survived it.

He was gentle and strong, tender and firm, generous and just. His love could say, No. His courage could yield. His frankness was never unkind. His sympathy did not degenerate into pity, nor his sweetness into sentimentality. He was meditative and practical, dignified and simple, vigorous and patient.

These things represent the miracle of character according to which men have called him divine. They are not dependent upon signs and wonders, nor the deliverances of councils, nor the edicts of courts, nor the acceptance of tradition. They are the simple currency of every land and age. No man is too simple to understand, no man too great to obey.

Thus he embraces the world—prince and peasant, East and West, rich and poor, ancient and modern; childhood, youth, maturity, and age. All sects claim him, all parties accord him honor, and those of no sect or party call him Lord or long wistfully after him. He is the perennial Problem and the perennial Master. One of the most significant developments of modern times is the demand, that Orientals are making now, that they have him, freed from Western civilization and the Western Church.

In a word, the power of Jesus rests upon the

breadth of his nature, by which he responds to the need of men. But the need of men is God. We must go further, then, and say that the power of Jesus is in his possessing and purveying God to men. He showed men God, and when they touched him he gave them God—God, the Lover of men, the Sufferer with men, God, who had borne the Cross always in his heart.